Beating about the Bush
A History of Hertford Heath

by Pam Kimpton

Rockingham Press

Published in 2008 by
The Rockingham Press
11 Musley Lane,
Ware, Herts SG12 7EN
www.rockinghampress.com

British Library Cataloguing-in-Publication Data

A catalogue record for this book
is available from the British Library

ISBN   978-1-904851-25-7

Printed in the United Kingdom by
Biddles Ltd,
King's Lynn
www.biddles.co.uk

I dedicate this book to my mother,
Violet Newton, who was
born in Hertford Heath, as were
her mother, grandmother
and great grandmother.

Bibliography

Domesday Book

Pond Dipping   The Women's Institute

Hertford Heath: History of A Village School   Kenneth Rimmer

Haileybury Since Roman Times   C.M. Matthews

The Life of Florence Barclay   by one of her daughters

Kelly's Historical Directories   1890 to1914

Hertfordshire Inns   W. Branch Johnson

Late Bronze Age Artefacts   Clive Partridge

The Late Place-Names of Hertfordshire   J.E.B. Glover, Allen Mawer
                                                      and F.M.Stenton

Hertfordshire Yesterdays   Frank Ballin and
                                                      Malcolm Tomkins

Foreword

My childhood spent growing up in Cuffley gave me a taste for village life. As a wartime child, I can well remember the class relocating to air raid shelters for *Tales of Milly Molly Mandy*. The senior boys collecting doodlebugs from the railway and gasmasks kept in the cupboard on the landing. It has left me with an enduring love of the countryside, appreciation of the seasons and the enjoyment of simple pleasures.

Raising my family in Springle Lane introduced me the area around the Heath. We discovered carpets of primroses in Hailey Woods and a favourite outing was to the Haileybury pigs, feeding Lillian with Polo Mints and marvelling at the cutlery mixed up in their swill.

We watched the A10 taking shape and searched the roadworks for flints and fossils. Little did I think then that I would end up in Toms Cottage in Downfield Road, changing from midwife to artist and doing a stint as Chairman of the Parish Council. At last after twenty five years, I feel less of a new girl.

Picnicking with the grandchildren or sun-basking on the green is my idea of heaven. It was there that Jean Bray would stop to chat. Now in her eighties, she reminisced about growing up in a cottage, the cramped conditions, lack of amenities, living off the land and surviving bitter winters.

Her stories made me eager for more so that when Pam suggested a history based on personal experience I encouraged her to go ahead. It proved to be a marathon task spanning the two great wars. Documenting a period of rapid change.

Thank you Pam for listening to their stories, retrieving their photos and piecing it all together in a patchwork of memories. *Beating about the Bush* will give pleasure to young and old. Serving as a reminder to each generation of the people and events which have gone before; and that the community we love is rooted in History.

February, 2008   Mary Bourne

A Map of Little Amwell, dated 1923

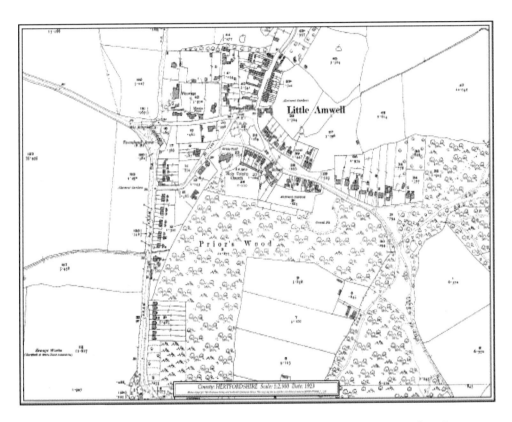

A large expanse of Priors Wood and the four fields before housing developments have taken place

Introduction

I did not realise how much history was associated with Hertford Heath until I started my research and hopefully I have uncovered most of it. The village has developed through the years, resulting in a community we can be proud of.

Recognition of the hard work put in by the Parish Council and the residents of the village came with the award of Hertfordshire Village of the Year East 2006, and following that in 2007 the prestigious prize of Overall Winner for Hertfordshire Village of the Year.

Members of the Parish Council that presented the village to the organisers of the 2007 competition were: Mary Bourne, parish council chairman, Bob Akers, vice-chairman, Carolyn Morgan, parish clerk and district councillor William Ashley.

The other members who played an important part were: Lyn Bonner, Trevor Goodingham, Gillian Thornton, Andrew Crumpton, Martin Nash, Jack Eames and Alison Scarll.

The contest was organised by the Campaign to Protect Rural England (CPRE). The Hertfordshire Society awarded a Plaque and a cheque for £250 to the village competition committee, at the County Hall in July 2007.

The village was judged on six categories: community life, business, young people, older people, the environment and information communication technology (ICT). A further prize, the Dorothy Abel Smith Award, was made to two Hertford Heath Primary School pupils, Edward Dukes and Chloe James, for making an outstanding contribution to village life.

My thanks to the people of the village who I plagued with questions and begged for photographs, all of whom I owe my gratitude to, as I could not have completed this book without their help. Many contributors completed questionnaires about times past when the village was small and living conditions basic. However there was always great community spirit and the village was largely self sufficient with local shops and businesses. Many people commented on the freedom of local children playing in the local woods and fields.

Since then the village has grown to twice its size and all that have moved here enjoy our way of life, and we welcome them in to our community. Some have played an active part in our Clubs and Societies and joined the Parish Council.

In particular I wish to thank my proof readers Bob Frost, John Cutler and Bob Akers for their help and patience, and Mary Bourne for her inspiration. Also Len Kiff, Victoria Sheppard of Haileybury Archives and the staff of Hertfordshire Archives and Local Studies (HALS).

Questionnaires were given to villagers who were born in Hertford Heath to provide an insight into their lives from birth on to school days, marriage, and their thoughts on how life has changed over the years. Many of them have stayed on the village all their lives and never wish to leave. This is the story of just of one of them.

Bubbles Broadwood

Bubbles (Margaret) Judd was born in 1920 and her first home was at No 2 Woodland Terrace, The Street, Downfield Road (the Terrace is no longer there).

She was one of seven children and the house was so small they slept three, sometimes four to a bed. There was no bathroom only a toilet block at the top of the yard with a wash house which was shared with neighbours. Clothes lines strung across the yard were also shared. The only form of heating was a coal fire in the living room. Meals in those days were stews without much meat, bacon dumplings, meat puddings, sausages and mash which is still a favourite today. Spotted dick and jam roly poly were the usual desserts. Breakfast was porridge, with teatime consisting of bread and cheese or jam, another good old standby was bread and dripping. Favourite sweets from the local shops were gob stoppers, bull's eyes, and sherbert daps.

Dr. Lemprière at Haileybury College was the family doctor. As her mother and father both worked at the College it was quite usual in those days to have the college doctor for the family practitioner. The vicar at that time was the Rev. P. Fear and Sunday school was a must to give mothers time to catch up with the housework. The local midwife was Nurse Camp, although any local woman who gave birth would get support from the neighbours who would rally round and help with the washing cooking and looking after any other children in the house. Nurse Dean was the school nurse succeeded by Nurse Dennison.

When someone died Mrs Rose Webb who lived in the Street would come to lay the person out ready for burial.

Clothes were bought from market stalls, jumble sales or from door to door salesmen who were paid weekly. Holidays and day trips were unheard of, times were hard. The family always kept pet dogs, cats and rabbits. Bubbles father had an allotment as there were no gardens in Woodland Terrace. When the family moved to Church Terrace they kept chickens and ducks which swam on the pond on the Village Green. Cows used to graze on the green and drank from the pond. The fountain on the green used to work then and there was a metal cup attached to it by a chain.

During the school holidays recreation time was spent making houses in the woods. The children took bread and jam sandwiches with bottled tap water to drink and there played all day. When blackberries were in season they were gathered and sold door to door *anything to get from under mum's feet*. The Amwell river was the only place they could swim until Haileybury College later allowed its swimming pool to be used by children of the staff in the summer holidays. Winters were severe but it usually snowed and the pond on the village green froze over. Sliding on it and playing in the snow was enjoyed by all the children in the area. Also Foxholes Hill was excellent for sliding down sitting on an old tin tea tray.

The Old School in Mount Pleasant had 20 – 30 pupils to a class and Mr. Thomas was Headmaster, followed by Mr. Williams. There was corporal punishment in the school using the cane. Running and later netball were the only school sports in those days. Playtime at school was spent skipping and playing marbles. Children spent all of their education at Hertford Heath School until the age of fourteen.

When Bubbles left school, she went to work in the kitchen of Haileybury College and earned eight shillings a week, but lived in. Later she went to work at County Hall, and then became manageress at Sketchley's Dry Cleaners in Hoddesdon. Her last job was at Merck, Sharpe & Dohme in Hoddesdon. Her mother, brother and three of her sisters all worked for some time at the College. She married Bob Broadwood whom she met at a dance in Tewin Village Hall. They lived in Woodland Road and had one child, Roger. Bubbles now lives in a bungalow in Oak Tree Close. Below are Bubbles' own words, written at the end of the questionnaire:

I had a happy and loving childhood. We lived in a two-bedroom cottage, I was the youngest of seven children. We didn't have much money and my parents worked very hard to bring us all up, but we always had enough to eat, plain food but nourishing. We had a wireless (a crystal set at first) and my sisters and I used to act out little plays that we invented in our bedroom. My brother being the only boy used to steer clear of us and did his own thing. We had a happy time, but sadly my mother died when she was only fifty years old after a long illness, but my older sister mothered me.

I miss the old days because of the freedom of playing and walking where you like and never having to lock the door; we trusted our neighbours absolutely, and enjoyed warm friendships with everyone in the village.

I have lived here all my life and wouldn't want to live anywhere else.

Contents

Insert of nine colour illustrations ....between pages 96 & 97

CHAPTER ONE

Hertford Heath (Beating about the Bush)

Hertford Heath (or just simply "the Heath") was just a wild wooded wasteland, mainly used as common pasture, with the Roundings known as the Great Heath and the area around the village green the Lesser Heath. The Great Heath was the best open land. In Hertfordshire the word Bushes was often used for sparse woodland with few large trees, perhaps this is where the nick name for Hertford Heath of "The Bush" came from, or because it was in close proximity to Hailey Bushes. Bus conductors in later days would always announce the arrival of the bus at Hertford Heath with the words "anybody for the Bush" and sometimes followed by the quip "watch out for the Indians". Another name given to the villagers was the "Bush Rangers".

The village of Hertford Heath only came into being with the arrival of the East India College at Haileybury in 1806. But the settlement has a long history going back to the Bronze Age, as evidenced by axes discovered in Priors Wood.

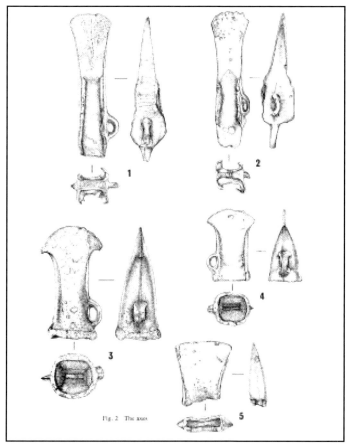

Drawings of the Bronze Age axes found in Priors Woods recorded in Hertfordshire Archaeology, *Volume 7 1979 by kind permission of Clive Partridge.*

The Bronze Age tools were found by Brendan Gannon, a local metal detector enthusiast, in the vicinity of Priors Wood (now Oak Tree Close) in 1977 and 1978. The collection comprised two complete winged axes, two complete socketed axes and part of another socketed axe; five fairly complete bun ingots, thirteen large fragments from bun ingots and six smaller pieces. Some were found in small bowl-shaped pits along with blackened stones and sooty soil whilst others were found as surface scatter in the same woods. This material has been acquired by the Hertford Museum.

There was a settlement of the Catuvellauni tribe here before Julius Caesar invaded in 54BC, and in 1956 when builders were digging prior to laying concrete for the garages in Trinity Road, an Iron Age Belgic chieftain's cremation grave, dating to the second half of the first century BC was found. Trinity Road was built on a field once called Grimstead Haw, suggesting that the Saxons who gave it that name had found awesome remains of a forgotten people who had once lived there. The first findings unearthed by the builders were a quantity of rusty curved iron bars, possibly from an iron bound chest, and a Roman amphora. These were sent to the British Museum and after careful examination were reported to be those from a British Chieftain's grave. The ground by then had been concreted over for a wash-down for cars by the garages.

The Hertford Rural Council, impressed by the accumulated evidence, generously allowed their concrete to be opened up, and on a hot July day the first sledge-hammer blow was struck by the builder who had found the first amphora. All that week villagers stood or lay on the blistering concrete peering into the cool pit where more iron, crumbling green bronze studded with crimson enamel, pots broken and unbroken, a handful of burnt bones, two tazza cups, 14 enamelled studs, six wheel-turned native pots in typical colours of black, red and brown, 21 pieces of decorated glass, an iron knife with a 9-inch blade, a pair of iron sheep shears 10-inches long, and the green glass bowl (bright as new but in pieces), said to come from Syria, returned to the light to be boxed in one of the garages and later laid out on the schoolmaster's dining room table for archaeologists of European renown to inspect.

The Haileybury Archaeological Society, led by Mr. G. Ridsdill Smith, spent the

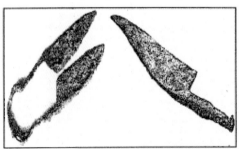 

On the left the shears and iron knife; right the glass bowl. The shears are the only ones yet found in a pre-Roman grave in Britain and suggest that there owner's wealth lay in sheep rearing.

next autumn and spring digging exploratory trenches round the concrete base of the garages to locate any encircling ditch near the grave and found the cross section of one in several places, three foot deep. Three other cremations outside the ditch and one within 50 yards of it were also found. Also scattered all over the area were coarse bits of pottery indicating an Iron Age settlement before the Belgae came. The British Museum said the find was of National and even International importance.

Each tenant that was allocated one of the garages from E.H.D.C was presented with a map highlighting the site of the Belgic grave and a certificate by order of the Minister, Mr. A.L.Little, pictured below.

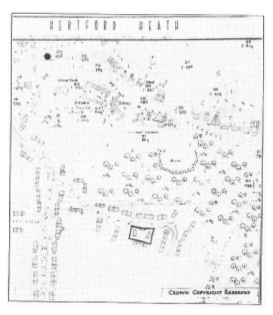

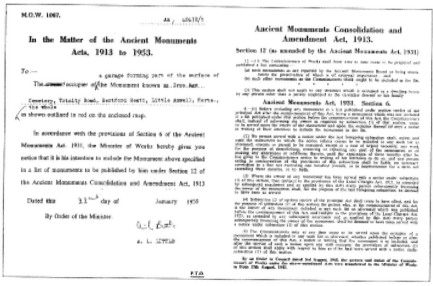

The Entry in the Domesday Book
for Great and Little Amwell

Although Hertford Heath itself was not in existence in 1086, the surrounding area that was Great Amwell and Little Amwell is recorded in this section of the book. This area included parts of Hertford, Hoddesdon and Earl Harold's manor at Hatfield Broadoak. All of these were probably included in the 14½ hides at Amwell. Earl Harold was, of course, King Harold who met his fate at the Battle of Hastings. The survey was commissioned at Christmas 1085, when William the Conqueror held court at Gloucester. In Hertford Hundred, Ralph de Limesi was granted the Manor of Amwell by William:

Ralph himself holds (Great and Little) Amwell. It is assessed at 14½ hides. There is land for 16 ploughs. In demesne (are) 7 hides (about 120 acres), and there are 2 ploughs, and there can be another 2. There 24 villains with a priest and 4 Frenchmen and 7 bordars have 8 ploughs, and there can be 4 (more). There are 19 cottars and 2 slaves, and 1 mill rendering 6s., meadow for 16 ploughs, pasture for the live-stock of the vill, woodland for 200 pigs, and from pasture and hay, 10s. In all it is worth £14.10s; when received, £12; TRE £18. Earl Harold held this manor.

The meaning of terms:

Hide:	the standard unit of assessment to tax, especially Geld.
Demesne:	Land 'in Lordship' whose produce is devoted to the Lord rather than his tenants.
Bordar:	a cottager.
Cottar:	also means a cottager.
Mill:	a rotary engine driven by water, in most cases for grinding corn.
Vill:	the local unit of local administration at its lowest level: Geld for instance was levied on the Shire, Hundred and vill in that order.
TRE:	the formula commonly used in Domesday Book to indicate the position 'in the time of King Edward the Confessor.'

In 1588 the Spanish Armada threatened to invade England. Beacons twenty to thirty feet high of timber, metal and pitch were built on high ground from the south coast northwards, to be lit as signals when the invasion occurred. Three hill top beacons were in built in Hertfordshire, one in Graveley another in Therfield and a third in Little Amwell. A fourth was also built on the steeple of St. Peter's in St. Albans. The beacons did there work so well that the Armada never landed on our shores. The beacons were repaired from time to time until the civil war was over. The Little

Amwell beacon lasted the longest out of the four, but was repaired in 1609 and 1622. But in 1626 it was ordered to be set up again. It was underpinned to the cost of £35.4s.7d. For all this trouble and expense, in 1702 the beacon was blown down in the great wind. The chief constable was then ordered to sell it for the best price he could get. The exact place is disputed but the village green part of the area called the Lesser Heath is the most likely position.

In much later years, one of the fields at the back of Amwell Place Farm was called 'Beacon Field' or 'Bonfire Field' because the Coronation and Jubilee bonfires were always lit there to celebrate the occasion. Beacon Hill was the former name for The Vicarage Causeway.

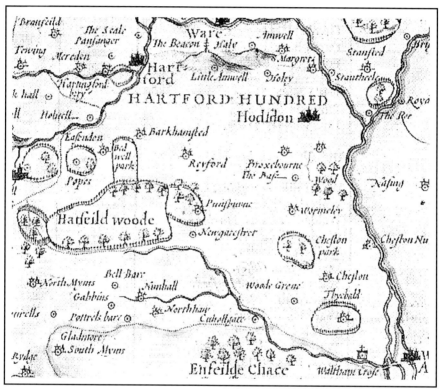

Part of a map dated 1676 showing the Beacon in Little Amwell, part of the Hartford (Hertford) Hundred.

The village in the early 1900's consisted only of London Road, Hogsdell Lane, Vicarage Causeway, Church Hill, Mount Pleasant and Downfield Road. Over the years there have been many new developments built including Woodland Road, Trinity Road, Trinity Walk, Oak Tree Close, Rushen Drive, Postwood Green, and Heathgate and The Harlings. The population has increased rapidly with these arrivals and the 2001 census showed that there were 2,549 people registered as living in Hertford Heath, of those 1,373 were males, and 1,176 females.

Running through the village was Ermine Street, a Roman road, originating in

London, which passed over the Roundings and continued from Hertford Heath Motors to the Townshend Arms, across the fields to Rush Green and on to York.

From the 12th to the 17th century the main road from London came past the present site of Haileybury College, which is now the small path that runs along in front of the main gates of the college, across the Heath, along Mount Pleasant past the village green, and down to cross the Roman road at the site of the war memorial and on to Hertford. The route was famously used when Queen Elizabeth I moved Parliament from London to Hertford during the plague years and you can picture the regal dignitaries as they journeyed across the muddy, rutted heath.

In 1630 a new road was ordered to be laid by the authorities across the Heath from the top of Hailey Lane at Highwood to the Roman road, of which a quarter of a mile came into use again. The only building along the road from Hoddesdon to Balls Park, Hertford, was the Jolly Pindar, an old tarred ale house. Legend has it that Dick Turpin in the 18th century lurked hereabouts.

Grimstead Wood adjacent to Grimstead Field was later renamed Priors Wood because the land was enclosed in Norman times and given to the Manor of Hertford Priory. Later it was part of Balls Park Estate. The land from here towards Ware and Hoddesdon belonged to the manor of Hailey. Lord John Townshend of Balls Park, at the other end of the village, let much of his land be enclosed and used for building from about 1800. Before that, Balls Park owned much of Little Amwell.

Little Amwell was formed from the parishes of All Saints, St Johns, and Great Amwell in 1864: with the building of Holy Trinity Church in 1863 it formed a separate civil and ecclesiastical parish from 1864.

For nearly 100 years, the village of Hertford Heath was split between two civil parishes, Little Amwell and Great Amwell. Little Amwell parish was wholly contained within Hertford Heath but the parish of Great Amwell covered the village of Great Amwell, parts of Ware and Hoddesdon, as well as the southern part of Hertford Heath. This meant that Hertford Heath's matters were considered by two separate parish councils. After much campaigning within the village, the two halves were finally united in 1990 under one Parish Council – Hertford Heath.

CHAPTER TWO

A brief history of Haileybury College

With the building of Haileybury College came a large movement of population from Little Amwell to Hertford Heath, as shown in the figures of the 1801 and 1811 census. Much needed work for labourers and servants, grooms, and gardeners, cooks and waiters was generated by its arrival. Cottagers of the Heath and the villagers of Little Amwell were bitter at first about enclosing of the common land but it was they that profited most as they moved into the college or to the new cottages in Hailey Lane.

In 1801 there were 403 people in Little Amwell living in 78 houses. In 1811, two years after the opening of the college, there were only 243 people in 38 houses. Meanwhile the population of Great Amwell, which included the college and Hailey Lane, had risen by 300. Forty houses perhaps ancient hovels were pulled down, but the village was soon rebuilt to twice the size, in Victorian brick, it has continued to grow and flourish ever since.

At the bottom of Hailey Lane, opposite the entrance to Hailey Hall, stood the parish poor house, an ancient building of plaster and thatch whose roof was always leaking and the inhabitants were always in need of something. The house catered for the sick, the poor, orphans and beggars. With the new college there was the opportunity to collect enormous rates without one new pauper to provide for. The old building was later abandoned and the occupants moved to a more suitable building in Hoddesdon.

In 1805, the rich and famous East India Company chose the site upon which stood the old Hailey Bury House, previously called Hailey Bushes on the edge of the Heath, for their college to train civil servants for the company's empire in India. The Castle in Hertford was also considered, but the accommodation was not sufficient. It was decided to use the Castle temporarily whilst the new college was being built. The house and estate, which were owned at that time by Dr. William Walker who had served twenty five years in Bengal, was put up for auction and was sold at auction to the East India Company for £5,900. The estate of Hailey Bury was fifty-nine and a half acres. However, the East India Company wished to have an imposing entrance on the main road so the four fields which lay between Hailey Bury and the main road, belonging to the Manor Farm and part of the demesne of Hailey, became the property of the Company.

The college was founded in 1806 and took three years to complete. William E. Wilkins was the architect and designer, and this was his first big commission at the tender age of 27. He went on to build the National Gallery in Trafalgar Square. Wilkins created his buildings in a neo-classical style round a large grass quadrangle (still said to be the largest academic quadrangle in the land). The building cost in excess of £50,000. When bricks were needed for the building of the college, the first Principal, the Rev. Samuel Henley, looked around for suitable clay. He found this in Hogsdell Lane, in two fields which he bought, so part of the College was built with Amwell bricks. The last house to be built with these yellowish bricks was Crossways in Vicarage Causeway.

Two of the first distinguished masters were the Rev. T.R. Malthus, R.F.S., who was a Professor of History and Political economy, and the Rev. Joseph Hallett Batten, a Professor of Classical and General Literature. The building could accommodate 100 students, and each paid 100 guineas a year for board and education, and a further 100 guineas on leaving for the benefit of using the library.

In the 1850's the East India Company realised that their days were numbered, debates in Parliament ruled that the East India Company's control of India could not continue, mainly as a result of the Indian Mutiny. In 1855 an act was passed "to relieve the East India Company" of the obligation to maintain a college at Haileybury. Its first clause stated that the college should be closed in January 1858. It was a sad day to close half a century of great distinction. It was also a sad time for the Honourable East India Company, which was dissolved shortly after the closure of the College.

The buildings stood empty for three years and the grounds stood desolate until in 1861 the government sold the property at auction to a speculative land company for £15,000. In the following year Mr. Stephen Austin, of Hertford, who had been printer to the East India Company, mounted a campaign to launch Haileybury as a new public school. He approached some leading church personalities and land owners, including Baron Dimsdale, to form a new Board of Governors. After some debating and disappointments, they purchased the estate for £18,000 and the new school was born. The new public school opened for the first time on 23rd September 1862 with the Rev. Arthur Gray Butler as the first Head Master. A Royal Charter was granted two years later and Haileybury soon became one of the best known schools in England. In 1874 one of its masters was appointed head of the United States Services College at Westward Ho in Devon. It later moved to Windsor under the name of The Imperial Services College. This set the connection between the two schools and in 1942, when the war caused a dramatic drop in the number of pupils at both colleges, they amalgamated as a financial necessity. The senior part of The Imperial Services College migrated to Hertford and joined with Haileybury.

The school grew fast, and in 1865 the old house, now for the first time called Hailey, was renovated and the dormitory wing added. The policy of the new Haileybury was to enlarge the estate and it now covers four hundred acres. The first addition was part of Goldingtons waste land owned by Mr. Cowper, between College Road and the main buildings. Other land and properties purchased were the cottage in the corner of Hailey Field, which had been a beer house, the cottages in Hailey Lane, built by William Wilkins at the same time as the college, and the orchard behind them. In 1881 the Quitchells (site of the famous Quitchell's oak), officially of twenty two acres, was added to the estate. Arthur Bloomfield's domed chapel was added in 1876, which became one of the best known architectural set-pieces in the County and gave Hertford Heath its defining skyline image. It overlooks the Rugby Pitch and the running track, where stands the oak tree called Lightening Oak. This particular tree is reputed to be over 500 years old and has been struck twice by lightening, the first time it was thought to have died only to be brought back to life by the second strike.

The In Memoriam board in the chapel honours former students who have played a major part in the life of the nation. One hundred and fifty six became generals, and others have risen to high rank in other services, seventeen have won the Victoria Cross "For Valour" and three more the George Cross. Also mentioned is Earl Atlee KG, OM, CH, PC, Mayor of Stepney in 1919 and Prime Minister, 1945-51. He was a regular visitor to his old school and unveiled the VC memorial on the Terrace. Nearly 1,000 Haileyburians died during the two world wars, including five masters.

Other famous Haileyburians are a recent Lord Mayor of London, Sir Clive Martin, Rudyard Kipling, Lord Allenby, Stirling Moss, Michael Bonallack, Alan Ayckbourn, Simon MacCorkindale, Lord Sainsbury, and John McCarthy.

Haileybury had strong connections with the services and many senior figures have houses within the college named after them, including Trevelyan, Bartle Frere and Allenby. For many years the college had large numbers of army, navy, and air force cadets among its pupils and one could pass through the college grounds and see the cadets on parade. Commanding officers lived in and around Haileybury, among them Major Denny, Mr. Jerrard, and CSM Bert Langman.

In November 1962, the Queen visited Haileybury on its centenary. The royal car turned into the school grounds from Hailey Lane at 3.15pm and came to rest on the running track below the terrace, in front of the chapel. Her Majesty was given a conducted tour of the college both by masters and by pupils, and asked that four extra days be added to the Easter Holiday to celebrate the occasion.

In 1968, the first girls joined classes at Haileybury. They came from Christ Hospital School in Hertford and studied Russian. The decision to increase the number of day boys was taken in 1980, and by 1987 there were sixty-six members. The lower school was started in September 1983 to admit eleven year old boys, previously educated in the state system. The numbers of pupils has been increased from 583 in 1995 to 743 in September 2006.

Looking back what has changed dramatically is what goes on within the buildings. In 1886, five hundred boys arrived at the start of the term, mostly by train, and many of them did not see their parents again until they left by train to return on the last day of term.

Hertford Heath residents received a shock when the first college closed as many lost their jobs and over half the village population worked there. However, with the opening of the new school many more jobs were created. They included work in the laundry, cleaners, porters, heating engineers, matrons, gardeners, laboratory assistants and work in the grub shop. Much of the college land was used for growing fruit and vegetables and so many more people were employed for this purpose. Large numbers of pigs were kept within the grounds and a pig man was employed, one of the last being Albert Jackson.

Many of these people spent their entire working lives at Haileybury and there is no doubt that this is one of the reasons for the special relationship between the college and the village.

Some of those with long standing service in the past have been Percy Chittenden, Frederick Gray, Jim and Winifred Locking, Charlie Evans and John Barrack. Bernard Budd, another great Hertford Heath character, is remembered not only for his long service but also for driving a horse and cart around the college and the village, amongst other things, to collect and deliver scraps for the pigs kept at the college. The horse was named Polly and was well loved by all.

Children of the staff were allowed to use the boy's swimming pool in the summer holidays and Christmas parties were given for them in December, starting with films in the Big Hall at 3 o'clock and a sumptuous tea in the dining hall. A Punch and Judy show was followed by games and Christmas carols. The highlight of the evening was Father Christmas emerging from the Kitchen Servery with presents to be handed out to everyone. Staff were also given free tickets to see the famous plays, operas, or pantomimes. Yearly outings to Clacton were also organised for staff and their children. These were called 'Pastimes'.

SWIMMING BATH, HAILEYBURY COLLEGE

The Haileybury swimming pool before the water slide was introduced on the left hand side, now replaced by a large indoor pool on a new site which is open to the general public.

Cecil Hudson, who was born on the Heath, remembers that "during the 1930s there was a good rapport between the college boys and us, we would meet in the woods, off twenty acre and supply them with cigarettes (Turban 10 for 2d), obtained from the machine outside the village shop, they in turn bringing us ice-cream and sweets from the tuck shop". November 5th meant 'guying' under the dormitory windows, boys would drop 'heated' pennies from the windows. "Sunday mornings during the same era, the boys walked down London Road, round by the church and up Mount Pleasant, through the 'coke path' in the Heath, back to the college, wearing their Sunday best, complete with 'boaters', us mischievous young boys would hide in the thickets and try to flick off the boaters with hazel sticks. We looked forward to the end of summer term when the leavers sold off their cycles, bats etc to 'dorm' men who in turn passed them on to us."

Many people of the village are still working at the college today; and many have been long serving, with some having generations of their family working there before them.

This is a staff photograph taken in 1962 in front of the memorial dining hall that was opened on 7th July 1932 by the Duke and Duchess of York (later King George VI and Queen Elizabeth). Some of the local employees are named here; unnamed staff members from outside the village are marked with '?'

Back Row: Bill Bell, ? ? ? ? Cyril Purlant, ? ? Alan Roberts, Fred Lingwood, Jim Brace, Charles Francis, ? ? John Stratton, Bernard Budd, Fred Porter, Les Foster, Harry Judd, Cyril Lewis, ? Reg Cox, ? ?

Second Row: George Camp, ? Susie Jordan, ? ? Amy Webb, Elsie Chittenden, Glad Howsden, Sara Timpson, Harriett Perry, Mrs. Locking, Dolly Golding (Phypers), Eileen Webb, Syn Rolfe, Jackie Webb, Dolly Akers, ??, Dolly Barwick, Elsie Bates, Ethel Hayden, Mrs. Pamphlin, Student Cook, Sylvia Race, Student Cook, Jim Brace, Mr. Jordan,

Third Row: ? ? ? ? Mrs. Seers, Mrs. Purllant, ? ? John Mannering, Bill Seers, Charles Evans, Ivan Porter, ? Tomasino-Vincent, Kitchen Staff ? ? ? ? Norman Middleton, Oscar the barber, Jim Locking, Bill Hillary, Jim Davies, ?

Front Row: Tom Sayers, Miss J Saint, ? Fred Rolfe, ? George Beaver, Leslie Tunnicliffe, Charles Powell, Revd Morgan, Dr Turtle, ? Christopher Smith (Master), ? Harold Pamphlion, George King, Reg Farrow, Mr. Charlton, Bert Langman, Fred Muncer, ? ? ? ? Chef Gilbert

Percy Chittenden Servant of Haileybury 1917-1982

Percy Chittenden (Chitty) was one of the college's longest serving workers. He wrote his memoirs and some of them were published in the Edmonstone Magazine in 1960. He called them "Recollections of Haileybury" – here are just some of them.

I was just 12 years 7 months old when I came to work at Haileybury for the weekly wage of five shillings. I had seen an advertisement in the "Mercury" for waiters at the college. I applied for the job, but had to obtain exception from school. The headmaster, Mr. Goody, lived up to his name and said I could leave. My first impression was of horror when I saw that all the windows had thick iron bars. The servant's hall, now known as Red House, contained a large dining room, a bicycle room, and a pantry downstairs, and the upstairs were used for dormitories.

I began by being a 'Gally' boy, doing all the odd jobs, I was under Mr. Saggers who was head waiter in what is now the Reading Room where the tables were covered with table-cloths which, as a result of the laundry costs were removed during the First World War; then all the tables and benches had to be scrubbed every day. At the beginning of lunch Bill Blythe, the porter, who was an enormous fellow, used to stand at the door end when it was time; he gave a signal to the beak taking lunch, who then said grace. Bill used to go round making sure that all was well and taking notes on any points he thought fit, he was a truly memorable fellow.

What impressed me the most was the fire in the kitchen. It was about five feet high and fifteen feet long, where joints of meat used to hang from chains and there were pans underneath to catch the fat as it dripped off. While the joints were cooking someone was given the job of basting them

Percy Chittenden (in wheelchair) with former colleagues.

with fat from the pans. We could buy this dripping in 7lb jars for 6d. and my word it was good. In the Common Room (which is now occupied by organ works) they used to draw their beer up from the basement by means of pumps which were fitted on the sideboard. The lunches were always four courses. On Sundays there was a choice of several joints of meat, at breakfast they always had pork pies. There were high teas which catered for rugby teams, they had steak & kidney pie, potatoes and peas followed by a pudding and tea to drink.

In 1919 I was given the job of tobying in the Elysium and attending the beaks in the Deanery. There were no baths, only foot baths. When some of the beaks returned after the war there was a certain Captain Campbell, who whilst taking silent reading one Sunday fell asleep. The boys decided to creep out and the last one turned out the gas light. Captain Campbell found out who had turned out the light and summoned him to his study and said "So you're the boy who turned out the light, thank you very much – I sleep much better in the dark"!

I came to Edmonstone in the summer of 1932 as house toby when H.D. Hake (whom I was to serve for 17 years) was housemaster. At one of the last dinners to be held in the actual house of Edmonstone, Mr. Hake got a handicapped boy to stand on a chair and demonstrate his skills with a yo-yo to the amusement of the rest of the house. Also in the house at that time was a fellow called Jala who was the son of an Indian Prince and who later became a Maharajah, he was painted dressed in all his robes by the art master, Mr. Blunt.

The same year 1932, I had just finished clearing away Mr. Hake's tea things, when who should come through the door but Queen Mary for whom I opened the door! She had come to look at the new dining hall just before the Duke and Duchess of York came to open it. The cricket pitches used to mown by a horse drawn mower, but the horse had to wear special shoes to prevent damage to the grass. Previous to this, village boys had been paid a small wage to dig out the daises with penknives, so ensuring good turf. Later on a gas driven machine was used, which had a great big cylinder to hold the gas.In 1933 the science laboratories were opened whilst R.L.Ashcroft was deputy Master. There was much walking in those days, no motor vehicles, and much riding.

These are only some of Chitty's memoirs, but he was highly regarded by the staff and the boys of Haileybury. His wife Elsie, who worked in the dormitories, was also among those with a long service history at the college. Many of the pupils kept in touch with him long after they had left Haileybury. Percy and Elsie were among those in the village who had kept goats, they also loved gardening and for many years Percy produced an excellent variety of home made wines. Their home in London Road was always open to the village people for a glass of wine with Elsie's home made cakes together with good conversation and plenty of laughter.

CHAPTER THREE

The Chapel and Church

The Chapel was built in 1900, the third to be built on the London Road site. The official name of the building was *Reynold's Memorial Church.* Dr Henry Reynolds was president of Cheshunt College for thirty five years during the latter part of the nineteenth century, and it was in his memory that the chapel in Hertford Heath was erected. The Chapel closed in September 1991 and was demolished in 1996 to make way for residential housing – see the photograph on the colour insert between pages 96 and 97.

Francis Johnson, a Professor of Sanskrit at the East India College founded the first Chapel in 1829 out of the profits of a Persian and Arabic dictionary that he had compiled. The second chapel was built in 1868.

Selina Hastings, Countess of Huntingdon, a great eighteenth-century evangelist, opened private chapels attached to her residences, which she was allowed to do as a peeress of the realm. These were used for public preaching of the gospel, but they become a source of contention from the local Anglican clergy, with the result that she reluctantly seceded from the Church of England in 1781. The first Ordination service in the Countess of Huntingdon's Connexion was held on 9th March 1781, during which the Connexion's Articles of Faith were first read. Over 200 chapels and Mission Stations, among them the Reynold's Memorial Church were set up by the Connexion. Another great institution that she founded was the Cheshunt College, and in 1967 it joined forces with Westminster College, Cambridge, moving there in 1967. The Countess of Huntingdon's Connexion supported a missionary service in Sierra Leone and despite the small membership of Hertford Heath Chapel they too contributed to this mission. Another worthy cause they supported was the Sunshine Homes for Blind Babies.

Five Ministers preached in the chapel during the 1900's and their names have been found in an old accounts book dating back from 1st February 1929 to December 1960. The first to appear in 1929 was Rev. F. Higgins, with Mr. W.J. Wheeler as Assistant Minister, Mr. W.E. Huson as Treasurer and Mr. H.Huson was the caretaker. Subsequent Ministers were Rev. Wolfe, Rev. D.S. Dakin, Rev. Simpson and Rev. Clegg.

Most of the services were conducted by Lay Preachers, students from Easney College, and members of their own congregation. Holy Communion was celebrated once a month. Marriages could not be conducted in the Chapel but funeral services could.

Reg and Mary Ashton

Mr. Reginald Ashton, the blind elder, appears in the book in 1944. He married Mary Nottage, also blind, the daughter of Mr. and Mrs. W. Nottage. They went on to teach children in Sunday School classes, and also on Wednesday evenings. Their home was called Hope Cottage in London Road, and all children that attended Chapel were always welcome there. They amazed everyone with the way they coped with their blindness. Reg conducted the prayers and Mary played the harmonium. Among those assisting were Harry and Mary Huson and Miss Sutton; Mr. Kershaw often came to assist with the sermons. The children enjoyed going to the Chapel, as amongst other things they were occasionally given tea parties which were followed by games.

From 1935 through to 1960, a Miss Webb was the cleaner. She was presented with a gift every year for her dedication. Mr. Fitch the local builder did all the repairs on the building, and Messrs Grundy & Co. dealt with the solid fuel boiler.

The last service to be taken was in 1991. Among those attending were Mr. Tim Wells and Mr. Andrew Goodman.

Today there remains only 23 chapels in the English Connexion, maintaining an evangelical witness in towns and villages, mainly in the southern half of England.

Holy Trinity Church

Holy Trinity Church was built in 1863, in the Early English neo-Gothic style, as the parish church of the liberty of Little Amwell. The Rev. David Barclay Bevan of Amwellbury organised the building and became the first vicar. The land was provided by Viscount Townshend, Lord of the Manor of Little Amwell.

The foundation stone was laid in 1862 by Mr. Robert Hanbury of Poles, Ware (now Hanbury Manor). The architect was Mr. Ewan Christian and the builder was Mr. Walter Hitch of Ware. The building and fittings cost just over £1,400, mainly funded by Mr. Barclay Bevan. The church was consecrated on 13th August 1863 by Bishop Wigram of Rochester, to which diocese the parish belonged. In 1963 the lych gate was built to commemorate the centenary. Until the church was built, religion used to be taught in the village school or the Countess of Huntingdon's Chapel on London Road.

Vicars of Holy Trinity:

David Barclay Bevan, M.A.	1863 - 1880
Charles Wright Barclay, M.A.	1881 - 1920
W.A. Rice, M.A.	1921 - 1927
P.J.J. Fear, M.A.	1927 - 1936

A postcard of Holy Trinity Church

Charles Neill, M.B., M.A.	1936 - 1938
R.C. Nicole, M.A.	1938 - 1939
L.C.F. Tomkins, M.A.	1939 - 1943
H.C. Hargreaves, M.A.	1943 - 1952
Herbert Reseigh, A.K.C.	1952 - 1955
Charles Ellis, M.A., M.B.	1956 - 1972
John Budd	1973 - 1996
Marion Harding	1996 - 1997
Roger Bowen	1997 - 2004
Nicholas Sharpe	2005 -

The Church and the Barclays

The Rev. C.W. Barclay and his wife, Florence, lived in the Old Vicarage in Hogsdell Lane; they kept a very large staff, carriages and horses, coachman and groom. Later came the cars and chauffeur and under-chauffeur, gardener and under-gardeners. In the paddock there was a long brick building called the laundry and several women were employed there, purely for the vicarage use. They also kept their own dairy herd in the field opposite the Old Vicarage, which was owned by Rev. Barclay. School sports were sometimes held in this field. The dairy was a portion of the building at the far end of the vicarage. In the paddock there was a Scouts' hut, the scoutmaster being Mr. Carter who was assistant master at the village school and he too lived at the Vicarage. Later a large tennis court was built at the bottom of the vicarage gardens.

Nearly every household had its own well or shared one with a neighbour, and there was also a pump on the village green. However, in November 1897 the water supply was found to be "not safe for a public supply", its appearance being "turbid, yellow with much foreign matter and sediment". Rev Barclay, who was also the Chairman of the Parish Council decided to have a well sunk in his own grounds at his own expense, and by June 17th 1898 the artesian well was sunk in the vicarage paddock to a depth of 200 feet. It was operated by a wind pump which pumped water into two large tanks in the vicarage. Once these were full, the water was diverted to the reservoir on the village green, which apart from their own little wells in their gardens became the only source of water for the village. This was the position until water mains were installed. In addition a fountain was installed on the green in front of the present water pump for the use of the children.

Florence, the daughter of the Rev Samuel Charlesworth, became the Rev Charles Barclay's wife at the age of eighteen. After a honeymoon in the Holy Land, she and her husband settled down in the place where they were to live and work for forty years. In early October 1881 Charles Barclay preached his first sermon in Holy Trinity Church. Florence had a gifted personality, not only in her duties as a worker and organiser, but as a wife, mother and mistress of the household. She formed a men's bible class on Sunday afternoons. This proved to be a great success and before long the membership grew to over a hundred and included practically every man in the village. This class continued for nearly thirty years. Mrs. Barclay also set up a 'Mothers' Meeting' group teaching them thrift classes. She bought large supplies of material wholesale, and then retailed it to the women who paid instalments every week. Each had her own card to record payments and in this way the poor were encouraged to help themselves.

Florence also set up a group in Friday nights in the Mission Room to entertain the village men in an attempt to keep them out of the pubs. The programme included singing, poems, reciting Shakespeare, humorous readings by Charles Barclay and sometimes songs by other friends. However, it was her magnificent voice and playing of the violin that were enjoyed most. The villagers joined in enthusiastically and one of the favourite songs was Longfellow's "Village Blacksmith" sung by the real village blacksmith with his sledge-hammer over his shoulder. She later became a famous novelist and wrote twelve books, the most famous being *The Rosary* which sold over one million copies. She became a mother to five children one of whom wrote her biography in 1921 called *The Life of Florence L Barclay*.

The Vicarage became the focal point for the social life of the village. The grounds were extensive and were used for school treats and the celebrations for the Queen's Jubilee, for parties and races and firework displays.

Before Mr. Barclay, the Barclay Bevans were in charge, they lived at Amwellbury in Walnut Tree Walk, running between London Road and Hoe Lane (then known as Presdales Lane). It was their practice to drive up to church in two carriages to take the services, the family in one, and the staff in the other. The horses were stabled on the site now occupied by the Mission Room.

The triangle of green in front of the church and bounded by the Crossways hedge was enclosed by a post and single rail fence, which had to be painted every year – white rail and purple brown posts. The grass was tended by the vicarage

Charles and Florence Barclay
with their five children.

gardeners as a quality lawn. The path with its small white iron gates at each end and ditch alongside were well tended. Because of the constant pedestrian traffic, back and forth between the church and the vicarage, this path became known as the Holy Path and the trees on the green are known as Barclay's chestnuts. Portland Place opposite the path used to be called Sacrament Lane and had an entrance on the left that led to the Vicarage laundry.

HERTFORD HEATH PARISH MAGAZINE

Details from a Parish magazine dated 1915, printed during the First World War with the front page written by Charles W. Barclay:

My dear friends,

As usual I send you a New Year's greeting with much prayer that God's blessing may rest upon our parish this coming year. These are indeed momentous times. We cannot foresee what may be before us. Sometimes we may long that we could have a glimpse of the state of England in another year's time, but God in his mercy has with-held such knowledge from us, but we may be assured that all must be well, our times are in His hands, and whether suffering and loss shall meet us or not, we know that God is using England to put down the greatest menace to the welfare and freedom and peace of the world, and we can thank God that even at heavy cost, He so honours our land.

The closing message I would lay before you is- "Pray without ceasing."

Believe me,

Your affectionate friend and pastor,

CHARLES W. BARCLAY

REGISTERS

BAPTISM   "Suffer little children to come unto me"
    Dec. 2.   Annie Elizabeth, daughter of George and Louisa Locking

MARRIAGES   "Be married only in the Lord"
    Dec. 5.   James Fisher Geddes and Louisa Berry
    Dec. 9.   William George and Lillian Augusta Hurley

BURIALS   "Blessed are the dead which die in the Lord"
    Nov.26.   Robert Joseph Hayes, aged 21.
    Dec.1.   Rebecca Childs aged 73

KILLED IN ACTION
"Be thou faithful unto death, and I will give thee a crown of life"
    Nov.19.   Henry West, aged 25

CHURCH COLLECTIONS			£ s. d.
Nov. 22.	Morning.	Church Expenses	0. 15. 5½
Nov. 22.	Evening.	" "	0. 11.10
Dec. 6.	Morning Alms	....	1. 00. 8½
Dec.20.	Evening Alms	....	0. 16. 3½

SPECIAL SERVICES ON JAN. 3rd.
The third of January has been set apart by the Archbishops, at the direction of our King, as a "Day of Humble Prayer on behalf of the Nation and Empire in this time of war" May I urge that as many as possible shall gather to plead with out God. United prayer from the world over must assuredly bring down a might answer. God waiteth to be gracious, Services at 11 a.m. and 6.30 p.m.

Rev Charles Barclay's last letter to his parishioners before he retired:

December 1920

It is with a heavy heart I send out to you the last copy of the Magazine. It has now for 20 years formed a link between us and I only regret that for the first 20 years I had not introduced it. I have had the covers with all our local news bound in one large volume which will be kept in the Vestry. I think it will prove useful for those who come after to see what has been done here in time past.

I have experienced unvarying kindnesses from you, my dear parishioners. Wherever I have been during the past weeks, I hear words of regret that Mrs. Barclay and I must leave you, and this spirit was very wonderfully expressed at the great gathering in the school when so large a number, 300, I understood, sat down to tea and then presented me and Mrs. Barclay with the splendid gifts.

I rejoice that the Memorial Cross to our gallant men, who gave their lives in the War, has been completed and, by the time this number of our Magazine is out, will have been unveiled. At the moment we are preparing for a special service in Church on the afternoon of November 28th, hoping to secure a Military Band and a large Contingent of those who fought for us. The Cross has been erected with perfect success and certainly is the most beautiful one in the neighbourhood. It stands very conspicuously on high ground and can be seen for many a mile around. It will testify to all who pass by that Hertford Heath served our King and Country right nobly, for we sent upwards of 200 young soldiers from our midst, of whom 34 returned no more.

It had been my hope to come round to every house and bid each one a separate farewell, but this is now beyond my powers, and I beg that all whom I may be unable to see personally, will take my written assurance of affection. My thoughts will constantly go back to Hertford Heath and I shall often pray that God's richest blessing may rest upon the Village.

Rev. Walter A. Rice, 1922-27, succeeded the Rev. Barclay, and stayed for six years. He and his wife had been missionaries in Persia (now Iran) and had a difficult job taking over from the Barclays. This is a copy of the letter written by Rev. Rice to his parishioners in 1922.

THE VICARAGE,

HERTFORD HEATH,

January 9th, 1922

Dear Friends,

This letter would be unnecessary if we had a Parish Magazine. Having gone carefully into the question I find that even if 200 copies were taken every month and the price doubled, there would still be a considerable loss, so for the present we must do without it; and I am writing you this New Year's Letter instead, and take the opportunity of wishing you all every blessing in 1922. Besides this letter a copy of the " Fireside Almanack " is being left at every house, and I hope you will put it up somewhere and read the daily text and that it will be a bond of union between us all.

In looking back over the past year the outstanding event in the Parish has been the retirement of the Rev. Charles W. Barclay after his many years of devoted service here together with Mrs. Barclay, and the sudden home-call of the latter at their new home, Limpsfield Court, exactly four weeks after their departure. Mr. Barclay has not yet revisited Hertford Heath, but I hope he will do so before long and we can promise him a hearty welcome. The new Vicar was instituted on February 25th, by Bishop Hodges. The new portion of the *Church-yard* was consecrated on September 24th, by the Bishop of St. Albans, who delivered a most interesting Address.

The *Choir* has been reinforced by several adults and a number of school-children, and we hope for further developments in the near future. Mr. Thomas kindly acts as Choir-master. The *Parochial Church Council* is getting well under way and much helpful discussion has taken place at its meetings. The *Parochial Church Fund* (Church Expenses, Free-will Offerings, and Mission Room and Parish Fund, combined) closes the past year with a balance in hand over £30 after meeting all the ordinary current expenses of the ? and paying £32 odd to the Diocesan Board of Finance and the Central Church Fund, and towards certain necessary improvements in the Vicarage. These three are all credited to our parochial apportionment payable to the Diocesan Board of Finance, which was raised last year from £14/10/3 to £49/6/4. Even this result would not have been achieved but for the strenuous and self-denying exertions of many friends who helped to carry out a *Jumble Sale* in the Vicarage Garden, on July 7th, an *Indoor Fete* on Dec. 2nd, and the *Concert* in the Schools on Nov. 2nd, organized by Mr. Hylton Stewart with the help of other kind friends from Haileybury.

Some old friends have left the Parish, but others have returned to it and new ones have come ; and I doubt not that if we all pull together we shall be able, with God's blessing, to make good progress. Miss Chessel has has had a very serious illness : at the time of writing, however, she seems to have taken the turn and to be on the road to recovery, but it will be some little time before she is restored to her former health and strength. Since Mrs. Cobley left, Mrs. Tennant has kindly acted as Secretary of the *Women's Institute*, which continues to flourish and is doing a very good work.

The *Lads' Bible Class* is in abeyance for the present but we hope to re-start it before very long. A flourishing Branch of the *Young Peoples' Union* has been formed and is carried on with the help of a number of keen workers. Up to the present it has not been possible to start a *Scouts' Troop* owing to the difficulty of finding a suitable Scoutmaster after repeated attempts. Plans are being formed for sharing a *Parish Nurse* with Great Amwell, the last named generously offering to pay two-thirds of her salary. Financially the success of the scheme depends upon the regular payment of the weekly subscriptions. And I would appeal to all sympathisers to lend their hearty support and give the scheme a fair trial for the benefit of the whole Parish.

The *Confirmation* will be held at All Saints' Church, Hertford, on March 27th, and the Preparatory Class begins on the 18th inst. Before that date I shall be glad to receive the names of those who wish to be confirmed : any others who are undecided and wish to know more about it are invited to come and see me to talk it over.

A *Motto* is a good thing. It gives expression to our leading aims and motives and serves as a helpful rallying cry. I should therefore like to suggest the following as our motto for 1922 :— "*Ye were bought with a price : glorify God therefore in your body*" (I Corinthians 6.20). Christ has given Himself for you : He has purchased you with the sacrifice of Himself. Will you not show your love and gratitude to Him by gladly entering the service of your new Master, which is the only true freedom, and brings joy and peace ? There is nothing in God's sight more precious than a saved soul and nothing more beautiful on earth than the lives of God's faithful servants. And then, may it be your chief aim, to *glorify God*. (1) First of all, by living as His redeemed child and letting your light shine brightly so that all around may see it. Show your determination, God helping you, to keep your Baptismal promises and come forward for Confirmation if you have not already done so. 2) And because you cannot serve God aright in your own strength, I beg you to use diligently all the means of grace, to come often and regularly to the Lord's Table, and make Sunday very different from all the other days of the week by keeping it in no ordinary sense as a holy, happy day. God has promised His very special blessing to those who honour His Holy day by not merely making it a day of ease or pleasure but by using it for the high and blessed purposes for which He has appointed it. You will find what he says about it in Isaiah 58, 13, 14. A well-spent Sunday is the best preparation for a successful week. (3) Here are are some other ways in which you may glorify God. Don't let your place in Church be empty : every one who is present encourages others and helps to make the Service bright and hearty. Everyone can do some definite work for God ; and you should ask Him to show you what it is. We can all do our little bit to help forward God's work in this village, and make it a better and happier place for our having lived in it. *What is your bit ?* Will you answer that little question and see that you do it ?

Many may like to have a List of the Services, which is here given, and also a permanent record of the Baptisms, Marriages and Burials, which have taken place during the past year.

SERVICES.

Holy Communion, 1st Sunday, midday ; 3rd Sunday, Evening ; other Sundays 8 a.m. Baptisms, 2nd Sunday in the month, at 3 p.m. Sunday Services, 11 a.m. and 6.30 p.m. (6 p.m. in the winter months). Thursday Evening Service 7.30 in Church or Mission Room, as announced. Churchings, before or after any Service, or as arranged. Children's Service, 3rd Sunday, at 2.30.

The Old Vicarage – prior to the 1970's part of the Old Vicarage gardens was sold for housing and named Barclay Close after the Rev. Charles Barclay.

The 1922 Parish News (continued) – many of the people born in the village or who have lived there for many years will recognise some of these names:

BAPTISMS.

Jan. 30—Richard Prince.
Feb. 13—Maggie May Judd.
Mar. 13—Betty Bardell.
„ 26—Edith Mary Cooper (Privately).
May 8—Rose Mary Hornett.
„ 8—George Herbert Hornett.
„ 8—Dennis James Hornett.
„ 8—Edith Dorothy Victoria Turner.
„ 8—James Edward Hayden.
July 24—Olive Joyce Dedman.
„ 31—June Elsie Mead.

Sep. 11—Cecil George Kitching.
Oct. 9—Leslie Gordon Turville.
„ 9—Freda May Plumb.
„ 9—Gladys Marion Phypers.
„ 9—Vera Honor Joyce Ethel Williams.
Nov. 20—Ronald Philip James Clark.
„ 20—Roy Edward Dix.
„ 20—Gladys Violet Hayden.
Dec. 11—Poppy Evelyn Childs.
„ 31—John Frederick Hawkins.

MARRIAGES.

May 14—James Albert Lewis Clark and Emily Gray.
July 7—George Sidney Todd and Emily Mary Pigram.

July 30—Robert Webb and Edith Minnie Douglas
Dec. 26—Alfred Outtrim and Doris Evelyn Ives.

BURIALS.

Feb. 19—Thomas Judd.
Mar. 26—Joseph Cox.
June 24—Annie Elizabeth Hayden.
Sept. 29—Rose Gray.
„ 27—Septimus Allen.

Oct. 24—Henry Kemp Littleford.
Nov. 16—Mahali Hudson.
Dec. 14—Sarah Gearing.
„ 24—Matilda Akers.
„ 24—Horace Stanley Turville

The Rev. Fear on the right taking the choir on an outing to Clacton in 1934. Also in the picture are Mr. H. Law on the left with his son Ernie and daughter May in the centre. Others are Dorothy Law, Mrs. Bulley, Robert Sibley, Sidney Rider and Cecil Chandler.

Some facts and stories about former Vicars of Holy Trinity Church

Rev. P.J.J. Fear, 1927-1936, stayed for nine years, and he had also been a missionary. His wife used to run the Women's Fellowship on Tuesday afternoons in the Mission Room. Delicious teas were served, carried in state from the Vicarage by two smart maids.

Rev. Dr. Charles Neill, 1936-1938, was a doctor of medicine, besides being a priest, and both he and his wife were very musical. He stayed for only a year.

Rev. R. Capron Nicole, 1938-1939, also stayed for only a year. He said the Vicarage was too big and had four of the nicest rooms, all with beautiful views, removed.

Rev. L.C. Fellows Tomkins, 1939-1943, was with us for four years. His wife was an invalid but was a very sweet person. They had a brilliant son, Oliver, who became the world famous Bishop of Bristol. May Law, who lived in Hogsdell Lane, was a domestic for the Tomkins family; she was only fifteen at the time and remembers helping Mrs. Tompkins with her daily routine as an invalid. Harry Law her father

34

The interior of Holy Trinity Church in 1935. during the celebrations of the Silver Jubilee of King George V.

was verger and sexton to the Rev. Tomkins in 1940. Congregations were very small, partly due to the war; he had a very unfortunate accident in the church when somebody had left the flap open over the steps leading down into the stokehole and he fell in. Nurse Dean was in the church at the time and summoned help, but he unfortunately died of a heart attack the following day. Many mourners attended his funeral.

Rev. Henry C. Hargreaves, 1943-1952, was vicar for eight years. A tall scholarly man who would call at the local school once a week to conduct prayers at morning assembly. He always had a smile for the children

Rev. H. Reseigh, AKC, 1952-1955, was vicar for three years. He was a young man and had a cheerful and bustling personality. He was very much interested in reviving the choir which had dwindled from Florence Barclay's time. He unearthed some old surplices and cassocks, and, not being able to recruit many boys and men, formed a choir with a dozen girls, two women, one man, one boy (his own son) and himself as choirmaster. More boys joined later.

Rev. Charles Ellis, 1956-1972, a World War I veteran, was here for sixteen years. He was an Irishman, 61 years old when he arrived and 80 when he retired. At one time he had served as a missionary and he had also been a farmer, and that may be why he kept turkeys in the Vicarage garden during his early years at Hertford Heath. He was always trotting across the green or riding his bike with his two dogs, their leads attached to the handlebars, round the village saying "see you in church on

35

Rev. Charles Ellis with his trusty bike, talking to Miss Randall

Sunday" to any one he saw. He always stopped to speak to his parishioners, and he sometimes went to the local pubs where he enjoyed a pint whilst talking to the customers. He often brought his dogs to church on Sundays leaving them tethered by the church door. Occasionally one of them broke loose and would run into the church to find his master. There then followed a brief interval in the service while Rev. Ellis patted the dog, before calmly leading it down the aisle to the church door to tether it again. No one complained about the delay and most found it amusing. Amongst those serving as churchwardens and in other capacities during his term of office was Major Denny, another World War I veteran, who was on the teaching staff at Haileybury College and an officer in the College Cadet Force. Mr. Ronald Askew, another churchwarden, also played an active role in the village. Both men were respected and always ready to discuss in confidence the problems local people might have. Rev. Ellis's wife, Myra, supported her husband in his work and took an active part in village life.

A Poem very aptly describing Reverend Charles Ellis

Who starts each day with a toll of the bell?
Whose dog howls a chorus to the sound of each knell?
Whose shaggy grey dog patiently waits for his master
And makes his old bike travel faster and faster?
Who greets his flock saying "See you on Sunday"?
Who cuts the long grass from Wednesday to Monday?
Whose cure is iodine for every known ill?
And has never been known to take care of a chill?
Who spent his last birthday mowing the grass?

Who disregards all the years that go past?
Who numbers his friends among all sects and classes?
And wears on his nose little gold half-moon glasses?
I'm sure you've all guessed so I've no need to say –
It is Charles – who is ready by night and by day –
To give us a word of blessing and prayer
And all of our troubles are anxious to share.   *Anon*

Rev. John Budd, 1973-1996, was vicar for 23 years, although for the first 18 months John and his wife Jill and their children could not live in the village, as a new vicarage was under construction. The old building which had served as the vicarage since the 1860's was by the 1970's considered too large and uneconomic to maintain. John Budd coped with the difficulties of carrying out his duties whilst not living in the village extremely well, and of course it was with great relief when he and his family were able to move in to the new vicarage in 1974-75.

By this time the village had grown in size and Pinehurst Estate had been built on the old golf course, which adjoined Stanstead Road near Rush Green. This estate accommodated people who had relocated from North London. John Budd took this new estate under his wing as it was included in the Parochial Church Parish. With Jill's help he did a fine job in helping the new arrivals settle in to their new environment and encouraged them to join the church and other village activities. He also held services at the Pinehurst Community Centre and helped set up other organisations on the estate. In addition to his church duties, he became chairman of the Youth Club Committee, also attended the Village Hall committee meetings, and was also Chaplain to East Herts Hospital in Stanstead Road. He also served as Rural Dean for five years which increased his work load even further.

John and Jill did a tremendous amount of work during their time in the village, at Pinehurst and later part of the new Foxholes Estate before taking their well earned retirement. They still keep in contact with the people of the village and write regularly in the Parish Magazine.

Rev. Roger Bowen, 1997-2004, was with us for seven years. Roger and his wife Miranda left the parish to resume his work for the Church in East Africa, teaching in a theological college and taking services in local churches. He took over the role of Rural Dean which took his work beyond the parish boundary. Roger regularly visited residents that needed his help and also organised many discussion groups held in the vicarage and other people's homes.

Rev. Nick Sharpe, 13th September 2005 – Our latest vicar and his wife Rachel along with their children Michael and Eleanor have settled in, and are playing an important part in the community

The Mission Room

The Mission Room, or Mission Hall as it was also known, was built in 1882 in the Vicarage Causeway during the time that Charles Barclay was vicar of Holy Trinity. As mentioned earlier, it was used regularly by his wife Florence for her Bible classes, Mothers' Meetings and many other uses. It has continued to be used by clubs and societies throughout the years and is also for hire to the public for small parties and gatherings.

CHAPTER FOUR

The Village School

Hertford Heath village school for boys and girls was founded in 1837 as a National School and remained as such until 1947. The population of the village was just 360, Little Amwell was then in the parish of All Saints' Hertford, in the diocese of Lincoln. From the beginning the school was within the orbit of the Established Church.

The promoters of the school of Hertford Heath were three professors of Old Haileybury (the East India College) namely C.W. Lebas, W. Empson, I.A.Jeremie, and the curate of All Saints, Rev. W.R. Colbeck. They requested a £75 building grant on March 8th 1838. This connection of Haileybury with the school was to continue down the years with numerous managers (renamed governors in 1968). The school was intended to receive 75 boys and 75 girls. Parents were to pay 1d per child weekly; the Master and Mistress of the school were to be paid £50. The school was built on a site provided for by the Marquess Townshend. The school was licensed for public worship, as the village did not have a local church. At the weekend the schoolroom was used as a Sunday school in the afternoon and as a temporary church on Sunday Evenings. The five clerical professors of the East India College took it in turns to hold a Sunday service in the schoolroom. An extension was made to the school in 1858 and another in 1870 to the front of the school, the local builder William Gray was chosen for this project.

At some time the management of the school must have been transferred to the incumbent of Little Amwell, as in 1891 the second vicar the Rev. Charles Barclay was taking an active part in arrangements for adding an extension for 45 infants.

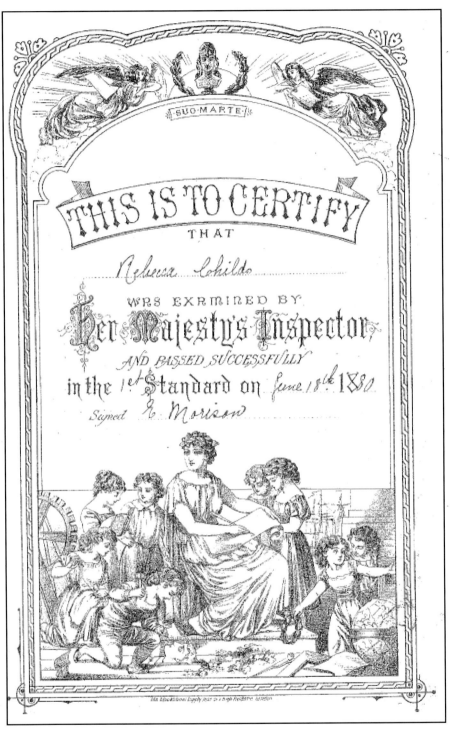

Certificates were awarded annually for pupils reaching the required standards adn signed by the school inspector, Mr E. Morison. This certificate was given in 1880 to Rebecca Childs, who lived in Downfield Cottage – she was the grandmother of Peter Ruffles, local councillor and former Mayor of Hertford.

The school remained a church school until 1947 when it became a State School, although it still remained closely linked with the Church. Harvest Festivals and Carol Services were held and the children helped with flower displays and produced a beautiful altar cloth.

William Chessell 1885–1915

The first recorded headmaster of the school was William Chessell. Mrs. Annie Chessell and her two daughters made up the bulk of the staff. Children remained at the school for all of their education until 1901, when secondary schools were introduced and children transferred to them from the age of eleven.

Mr. Chessell kept a meticulous log book in beautiful copperplate handwriting. In 1901 the log book shows that sickness and epidemics were a great problem in those days. Two cases of scarlet fever broke out in London Road on November 22nd but the Isolation Hospital was so full that they could not be removed. On December 9th, another case of scarlet fever was registered, Harriet Gray. This child was removed to the Isolation Hospital in the evening. In 1914 there was an epidemic of scarlet fever with twenty children from the school being infected. There were frequent outbreaks of measles, mumps, chickenpox, influenza, diphtheria, and scarlet fever, which continued until the early fifties.

Head lice were a problem first mentioned in 1911, when two children were sent home. Later there was to be a Nurse who would inspect the children for nits up to six times a year until 1945. The nickname given to the nurse was 'Nitty Nora' is still remembered today by some of the older villagers. Visits were made by the Dental Officer every few years.

There were always Attendance Officers on patrol, among them Mr. Thorne in 1915 and Mr. Bamber in the 1920's. Mr. Peet was well remembered as the Officer in the 1930's by pupils of that era. Beating the covers or bushes for different shooting parties was another reason for absenteeism from 1901. Boys were paid by gamekeepers to do this seasonal activity and it was to continue on for many years after this. Later in the 1930's, Mr. Ansell who lived at the Keeper's Cottage in London Road would give the boys 2/6d and a bottle of pop, bread and a quarter of cheese, for their services beating in Balls Park woods.

Mr. Chessell retired in 1915 after serving 30 devoted and faithful years. Mrs. Barclay, the vicar's wife, came to the school and gave very moving speech; she handed a letter containing a cheque to Mr. Chessell and her daughter presented Mrs. Chessell with a bouquet of tulips and lilies. Sadly, Mr. Chessell was to die only a few years after his retirement, in 1919. Twelve older children attended his funeral.

Mr. Chessell in his last year as headmaster, 1915.

The school house adjacent to the school was used for housing domestic staff in 1901. Mrs Annie Hayden and her husband were the caretakers of the school. Mrs Hayden is pictured here outside the school house with her two sons, James and John, and the family dog.

As can been seen in the photograph of the school pictured in 1933 there was a maypole in the school playground, and a bell tower. The school house can also be seen to the left of the picture. Among the children pictured here are: Gwen Turner, Barbara Mole, Brenda and Jean Dix, Rene Todd, Ginny Heeps, Bubbles Judd, Bob Akers, Joan Brown, Jack Hayden, Bob Beadle, Margaret Childs, Percy Cooper, Gladys & May Law, Bill Smith, Peter Pawley, Dorothy, May and Gladys Law, Sheila Atkinson, Billy Claridge and Aubrey Phypers.

Hertford Heath School in 1935. Back row: Bill Smith, Fred Camp, Dennis Hudson, Ken Kitching, Ivor Cast, George Brown, Peter Hindlough, George Fordham, Tony Gaylard and Mr. Thomas the headmaster
Front row: Denny Wilcher, Peter Parker, Stan Cutler, John Porter, Peter Childs, Robin Camp, Tony Barnes, Bill Brown and John Burgess.

Thomas Charles Thomas 1915-1943

Mr. Thomas was headmaster for 28 years, including a year and half of war service in 1917. One of Mr. Chessell's daughters was still a teacher at the school when Mr. Thomas became Head and both are remembered by some of the older villagers along with Miss Eva Night, Miss Susan Hurrell, Miss ('Thumper') Harold and Miss Milly Cox who were also teachers at that time. Mr. Naylor was deputy headmaster.

After Mr. Thomas's return from the forces, the school improved both in vigour and in promise of good work. Improvements were considered for the school. As there was some overcrowding in the main room of the school, it was thought that the caretaker's room would provide a room for practical work. This enabled woodwork for boys upstairs and cooking for girls downstairs.

Mr. Thomas was well known for being a strict disciplinarian and punctuality was taught to the pupils with his infamous words *"Punctuality is the soul of business"*. The main punishment at school was being given the cane. If you didn't hold your hand up, Mr. Thomas would bring the cane up from underneath, so that you got an extra hit.

In 1916 school gardening commenced as an ordinary subject. Pupils had to clear the woodland, donated by Haileybury, for use as the school gardens. This area is now known as Rushen Drive. This was an enthusiasm keenly promoted by Mr. Thomas. Older boys also worked in the allotments in London Road. Lessons in mothercraft were given to the girls while the boys were taught gardening. A footpath was cut from the school to the school playing field, the site of the present recreation ground. There cricket, football and athletics were practised. Mr. Naylor, the Deputy Headmaster, was a keen sportsman and he encouraged pupils to develop their sporting talents. During this time the school won many shields for athletics at the annual sports days at Hartham.

Mr. Thomas resigned on 17th September 1943 and the Managers wished him and his family many years of quiet and happy retirement. He retired to The Limes in Mount Pleasant; this has since been pulled down and two dwellings built on the site.

William Evan Williams 1943-1949 and
Myfanwy Williams 1949-1965

Mr. Williams was elected to be headmaster of the school in October 1943 with his wife Myfanwy as Supply Teacher. Mrs. Williams was his eventual successor. During this period schools were reorganised following the 1944 Education Act. Juniors and Mixed Infants remained at the Hertford Heath School and Seniors 11+s, were transferred to Hoddesdon Modern Secondary School, in Burford Street. Parents of the children were not pleased about this change and decided to revolt against it. Crowds gathered at the school, but Mr. Williams refused them entry, and refused to discuss it.

Another more radical change took place at the end of the Summer Term, 25th July 1947, when the Hertfordshire L.E.A. assumed all responsibility and the title of the school was renamed Little Amwell (Hertford Heath) County Council School. The school then had no further connection with the Church of England authorities. The managers had decided, after much uncertainty, to cease to be a National School.

Mr. Williams died on the 8th April 1949. The school closed for three days and re-opened on the 11th April with Mrs. Williams acting as head-teacher – she was appointed head-teacher on 19th July. Mrs. Williams was a strict teacher and was fastidious about her pupils coming to school each day with a clean handkerchief; this was to be shown at the pre-assembly line up. If it was not shown, you were sent home straight away to collect it. The author recalls: "This happened to me one day, I was on my way back to the school through Priors Woods (now part of Rushen Drive). I was about to jump over a puddle and saw a rather large grass snake slithering through it; I have never got to school so fast in all my life!"

Miss Eva Knight was still teaching at this time and is fondly remembered by all of the children she taught as a kind and helpful teacher, her patience was endless. She excelled at teaching the infants to read and write, with music being another favourite lesson. All of the children would want to play the larger more exciting instruments and not the dreaded triangle. Mr. Windebanks was another excellent teacher, but left to become headmaster at another school. Later Beryl Gibson, Mr. Evans, Miss Hall (Mrs. Risby) Mollie Walker, Mr. Proctor and Esme Nix joined the teaching staff. Before she became a teacher, Mollie Walker was invited to be a manager (as primary school governors were called then) in the 1950's.

The assembly hall had a big old coke stove in the middle with an enormous fireguard, and other rooms had open fires, also well guarded, which were barely adequate in really cold weather. Children were brought up from the back, a few at

Back row: Mollie Walker, Mrs. Williams and Esme Nix; front row: Mrs Risby, Ray Evans and Miss Eva Knight.

45

a time, to warm themselves. The assembly hall was used for school dinners. The teachers would help serve the dinners and Mrs. Beadle, a popular figure in the village, was among the kitchen staff. There were two playgrounds, one to the front, the other to the rear of the building The toilets were in the rear yard and in cold weather would freeze up, a place not to linger in any longer than you had too. Beyond the rear yard was a small field used for football, cricket and rounders. Nearby were some small allotments which had been cultivated in Mr. Thomas's time, but these were to be closed in October 1946.

The school became overcrowded in 1957 and it was reported that there were 145 children in the school in February. The school could only handle 100 pupils, but it was to be a decade before a new school was opened on 20th June 1966, just a year after Mrs. Williams retirement on 26th July 1965.

It was in Mrs. Williams' last year at the school that the ITA (Initial Teaching Alphabet) experiment was implemented, sponsored by the London School of Education. This was a controversial experiment, as pupils wrote as they spoke: *Wun* for *One, Woz* for *Was*, and so on. Most children found learning to spell by this method easy, but not all found the transfer to original orthography (TO) quite so easy; some took it in their stride but a few found it difficult. The experiment was to continue until 1980.

Bernard John Ashley 1965-1971

Bernard Ashley succeeded Mrs. Williams on 1st September 1965. He was formerly Deputy Head of King's Farm CP Junior School in Gravesend.

The new school in Woodland Road was still being built to accommodate the growing numbers of children in the area. Nursery classes were held in the old school building. Iris Ashley was appointed as Nursery Teacher, and Mrs. Smith as Nursery Nurse. To start with there were 20 children, attending on mornings only. Iris Ashley later taught infants in the new building with Biddy Butcher in the next class.

It was during Mr. Ashley's time as head-teacher that comprehensive schools arrived were introduced. Mr. Ashley was the first headmaster not to live in the school house (next to the school on Mount Pleasant). He chose not to rent this from the council but to buy a small house in Hertford, and the school house was then let. In 1971 the Ashleys moved on to a London Primary School, and Mr. Ashley became a successful writer of teenage novels.

David Smith 1972–1999

There was a gap of one term before the arrival of David Smith as headmaster, formerly deputy head of Broad Oak JM School in Hatfield. During this period, on 17th December 1971, Mrs. Nix announced her wish to retire after her eighteen year association with the School. She was presented with a bouquet and a cheque for £25, and the school staff later presented her with a silver ladle.

During Mr. Smith's headship the closer connection with the parents, started by Mr. Ashley, continued to expand and the Parent Teachers Association came into being early on. The PTA was responsible for much of the fund-raising, with activities such as discos, barn dances, car-boot sales, fêtes, fashion shows, wine and cheese parties and quiz evenings organised by enthusiastic parents. During the seventies Mr. Smith would take a group of older pupils for a week's sailing at Barton in Norfolk, and other popular resorts for visits with teachers have been Ironbridge, York, the Isle of Wight, and Llandudno. Maypole dancing was introduced, with the children giving displays on the playground, and the village green and at other schools.

Sadly David Smith died in 2006 and will always be fondly remembered by parents and all the children he taught. There is now a David Smith Award that is given to a pupil of the year who in the opinion of the teaching staff has consistently upheld the values and ethos of the school. David Smith was succeeded as head teacher by Mrs. Christine Wackett, who in turn was succeeded by Janice Smith.

Hertford Heath Primary School and Nursery currently caters for 170 pupils from three to 11 years old and has continued to have great success with its teaching achievements.

The new school in Woodland Road today.

CHAPTER FIVE

The Village Hall

Before the Village Hall was built, the School and Mission Room were used for village activities. However as the village grew it was felt that a larger and more modern building was needed to accommodate the swelling number of people and their activities. A suitable site was made available by Haileybury College. They leased part of Priors Wood, at a rent of ten shillings a year for sixty years to run from 25th March 1934. The rent was increased to £250 a year in 2004.

In 1933 a start was made to raise money for a hall. An extract from the *Hertfordshire Mercury* dated January 25th 1935 reads "friends and neighbours have rallied round and supported local efforts so generously that to date £800 has been raised by donations, dances, concerts, whist drives etc. The Carnegie Trust, through the kind offices of the National Council of Social Service, has made a grant of £225 and a further loan, for five years free of interest, of £500 was obtained." The building of the hall was well under way by this time, but the efforts in the village had still to go on to pay off loans and to raise more money to buy furniture. Even the children gave their pennies at school.

The Village Hall was built by a local firm, H. Fitch & Sons for the sum of £1,528.12s.10d. and was handed over on the 4th May 1935. It was built of yellow stock bricks inside and out, roofed with dark red double roman clay tiles and was designed to seat 200 people. This number has since been reduced to 100 to comply with present day safety regulations.

Meeting of the Building Committee No. 2

A Meeting of the General Committee was called on Thursday May 25th 1933 and met in the Mission Room at 8.30 pm.

All the elected members were present except J.Talbot Esq., Mrs. Wright, Sgt Major Copeland, Mrs.T.C.Thomas, Ch.Todd, F.Grover, Rev. P.H.Fear, Britcher, Mrs. Cronin and Mrs. Tennant. Most absentees sent explanations and expressions of regret at their inability to come.

Major Tennant was elected Chairman of the General Committee. He proceeded to outline the suggested organisation of the various Committees which would be necessary. After discussions the following <u>Building Committee</u> was elected: R.P. Atherton (Chairman) Major B.M.S. Foljambe (Bursar of Haileybury), J.Talbot, and Charles Drury.

It was decided that Major Foljambe should prepare plans and quantities and submit his suggestions at a general meeting to be held in July. In reply to a question, the chairman stated that no quotation, contracts, labour etc; would be settled until the General Committee had had the opportunity of discussing it.

The Chairman then asked the committee to approve the addition of several names to their number, as authorised at the General Inaugural Meeting. These were Dr. Lemprière, Mr. R.L. Ashcroft, and Mr. Lambert. This was approved.

Finance Committee was then elected as follows: Major N.R.D.Tennant as Chairman and Treasurer, Mrs. Talbot, Mr. Hawkins (Assistant Treasurer), and Dr. Lempriere.

A general discussion followed as to the best manner of organising the remaining members of the General Committee. The scheme to form them into a Helpers Committee dividing the district into areas, each under a 'Leader' was finally approved. Organisation as follows:

Hailey Lane	Mrs. Wright, Miss Sanderson, S.M. Copeland.
London Road	Mrs.Ch.Camp, Mrs. M.Camp, J.Webb, V. Hill, Mr. Williams (Leader of Group), Jordan, Suckling.
College Area	Mrs. Boxshall, Mr. J Huson.
Hertford Heath	Mr. H. J. Fitch, E. W. Bowers, W. Hayden, C. Watson, W. Mole, G. Cox, R.O. Sibley, E. Jaggs, E.Thurley (Leader of Group) and the following not present: T.C. Thomas (Ch. Todd)
London Road	F.Grover.
Woollens Brook	Mr. Britcher
Unattached	Mrs. Tennant, Mrs. Cronin, Rev. Fear, Mrs. Batchelor Russell, R.L. Ashcroft.
Secretary	Rev. C.H. Brown.
Ass Secretary	Mrs. Lambert.

Receipt books were issued to the Group Leaders and arrangements made for the systematic collection of donations and promises of support. Sums collected to be sent to the Assistant Treasurer and Treasurer periodically.

Mr. F.E. Hawkins expressed concern at the probable cost of annual upkeep but the general opinion of the Committee was that, if the Hall was built, means would be found to keep it going and that though a serious matter, it should not be allowed to hold up the main scheme.

Signed: N.R.D. Tennant. May 28 1933.

In June 1935 the Board of Charity Commissioners for England and Wales became the Trustees of the Hall and a Council of Management was set up to manage the Hall, consisting of ten members, seven from village organisations and three co-opted members. This council was then known as the Hertford Heath Village Hall Committee.

Major Tennant on the right with Viscount Allenby inspecting the Haileybury cadets.

Hertford Heath Village Hall was declared open on 4th May 1935. It was built to commemorate the Silver Jubilee of King George V and Queen Mary which was celebrated two days later.

Below: Major Tennant outside the hall looking at the crowds before the opening ceremony.

Sealed 21st June 1935.

2573

35

County - HERTFORD.
Parish - LITTLE AMWELL.
Place - HERTFORD HEATH.
Charity - HERTFORD HEATH
VILLAGE HALL.

A.
_____
115,959.

Order for
Vesting in Official
Trustee of Charity Lands.

Stamp 10s.

CHARITY COMMISSION.

In the Matter of the Charity called or known as the HERTFORD HEATH VILLAGE HALL, at HERTFORD HEATH, in the Parish of LITTLE AMWELL, in the County of HERTFORD, founded by a Declaration of Trust dated the 19th July 1934; and In the Matter of "The Charitable Trusts Acts, 1853 to 1925".

THE BOARD OF CHARITY COMMISSIONERS FOR ENGLAND AND WALES, upon an application made to them on the 24th May 1935, in writing, signed by

NOEL ROY DALCOUR TENNANT, of "White House", Haileybury, Assistant Schoolmaster;
CLIFFORD WALTER CRONIN, of "Heathfield", Chartered Accountant; and
CHARLES DRURY, of "Resthaven", a Captain in His Majesty's Army (Retired List); all of Hertford Heath, in the County of Hertford;

the Trustees of the above-mentioned Charity:

DO HEREBY ORDER as follows:-

The land and hereditaments specified in the Schedule hereto shall forthwith vest in "The Official Trustee of Charity Lands" for all the estate and interest therein belonging to or held in trust for the Charity.

SCHEDULE.

A piece of land situate at Hertford Heath, in the Parish of Little Amwell, in the County of Hertford, forming a portion of Priors Wood and having a frontage to the Main Road from Hertford to London together with the Village Hall erected thereon, held under a Lease dated the 18th July 1934 for a term of 60 years from the 25th March 1934 at the yearly rent of 10s.

Sealed by Order of the Board this 21st day

of June 1935.

L.S.

1030-20-5.

The Charity Commission order dated 21st June 1935

51

Crowds gather in 1935 to watch the opening of the Village Hall.

*One of the first flower shows to be held in the 1930's by the Allotment Society.
From left to right: Charles Morgan, Captain Drury, Bill Watson, John Howsen,
Mr. Bowers, an unidentified man, and John Kitching.*

During the first years of the hall's history, many dances and concers were held. The
Cricket Club, Football Club, Tennis Club, Keep Fit Club, Boys' Club, Women's
Conservative Club, Mothers' Union, Allotment Society and the Haileybury Grub
Shop all used the hall during the early years. Whist drives were also held. During the
war, evacuees were sent to the hall for dispersal and in September 1939 it was used
as an Air Raid Precautions Centre.

During World War II, a Home Restaurant operated in the hall. Below is the agreement for the restaurant, made in 1941.

THE HOME RESTAURANT AGREEMENT 1941

This agreement is made the ninth day of December One Thousand nine hundred and forty one BETWEEN THE CHAIRMAN AND TRUSTEES OF THE HERTFORD HEATH VILLAGE HALL COMMITTEE of Hertford Heath in the county of Hertford (hereinafter called "the Trustees") by MAJOR NOEL ROY DALCOUR TENNANT their duly authorised Honorary Treasurer and Agent of the one part and THE PARISH COUNCIL OF LITTLE AMWELL in the county of Hertford by PERCIVAL CHARLES GAYLARD their duly authorised Clerk and Agent (hereinafter called "the council") of the other part.

WHERAS the Trustees of the Hertford Heath Village Hall Committee have maintained and used the said Village Hall for the object of social welfare entertainment and benefit generally of the inhabitants of the Parish of Little Amwell and the surrounding district.

AND WHEREAS the Trustees gave the council permission to open a Communal Feeding Centre (to be known as "The Home Restaurant") in the said hall on the Twentieth day of October One Thousand nine hundred and forty-one and the Council are desirous of continuing to use the Hall during the continuance of the present war-time as such Home Restaurant.

AND WHEREAS the Council have agreed to pay the Trustees the sum of Ten Shillings per week during the continuance of this Agreement.

IT IS HEREBY AGREED as follows:

IN pursuance of the said Agreement and in consideration of the weekly sum of payment TEN SHILLINGS per week the Trustees herby grant permission and licence to the Council to use the said Village Hall as a Communal Feeding Centre during the continuance of the present war-time emergency subject to the conditions rules and restrictions set out in the Schedule hereto which said conditions rules and restriction are to be binding on both parties hereto.

AS WITNESS the hand of the Trustees by Major Noel Roy Dalcour Tennant the duly authorised Agent and Treasurer and the hand of the council by their Clark and Agent Percival Charles Gaylard.

THE SCHEDULE above referred to

1. The said payment of 10/- per week shall commence as from the 20th of October 1941.
2. The Council shall have the right to terminate the agreement upon giving one week's notice which shall be sufficient to terminate the same.
3. The Council shall have the right to remove any permanent fixtures fittings or appliances installed by them at any time (including the end of this Agreement) upon payment to the Trustees for any damage done to the building or its fittings and fixtures. Any dispute as to the amount of such damage shall be referred to the County Surveyor for his opinion whose decision shall be final.
4. The normal use of the building by the Council to be between the hours of 9 a.m. and 3 pm each day including Sundays but these times shall not apply in times of air raids threats of invasion or other national emergency. The Council to have permission to leave the Tables set except on specified days to be agreed with the Trustees.
5. The Council will not interfere with or damage the goods and chattels of other public or semi-public bodies which use the hall and in particular the Air Raid Precautions Service and the Women's Voluntary Service and The Women's Institute.
6. The Council will pay a proportion of the existing Ware Damage Part 11 contribution caused by the increase in value due to fixtures and fittings and chattels belonging to the Council attached to or left upon the premises.

7.   It is to be clearly understood by and between the parties hereto that if this building is requisitioned by the Government this Agreement shall absolutely cease and determine as from that time and no claim for damages or compensation shall be made by either party hereunder against the other (other than the right of the Council to remove permanent fixtures fittings or appliances as set out in Clause 3 supra).

Many organisations have used the hall. Among them the Girl Guides from 1941 (with one of the most memorable leaders being Mabel Foster) and the Boy Scouts in 1943; the Brownies joined the Guides in 1944. The British Legion held meetings from 1945 and the Women's Institute from 1947. Youth Clubs were introduced to the hall in 1949. The Hertford Heath Players put on plays and pantomimes from 1953.

Mr. Harry Fitch was President of the Village Hall Committee for many years, a post which has not been filled since he retired from the Committee. Major M.C.M. Denny was chairman in 1950 and Mr. P.C.Gaylard vice-chairman, Mrs. D. Janes treasurer and Mr. J.D. Smyth secretary. Another long serving chairman was Mrs. Joyce Wright of Mount Pleasant who served until 1977; she was succeeded by Harry Beardwell, formerly of Mount Pleasant, who served until 1995, resigning due to ill health. Harry Beardwell was supported by his wife and sister-in-law who both served on the committee. In Harry Beardwell's term as chairman, the 50th anniversary of the hall was celebrated. Among those that attended the evening together with Harry Beardwell and the committee were some of the people who attended the original opening ceremony in 1935. They included Mr. Vic Ansell, Mrs. Lily Bean, Mrs. Dorothy Chalkley, Mrs. Ethel Watson, Mrs. Kit Griffin, Mr. Arthur Bush and Mrs. Eva Hart. Also during Harry's term in 1986 the hall was awarded a Certificate of Merit for Hertfordshire's Best Managed Village Hall.

George Meekins, of Postwood Green, stepped in to help for four years in 1998, followed by the present chairman Dave Morgan, of London Road. Pam Kimpton (the author) has been the treasurer during the reigns of chairmen Harry Beardwell, George Meekins and Dave Morgan. Edgar Mascall, formerly of Downfield Road, ably audited the books from 1965 until his death in 2001. Paul Gulson, of Postwood Green, kindly took over this role. Many village people have given their help over the years to keep the hall functioning – they are far too numerous to mention individually, but all will be remembered for their assistance in a very worthwhile cause.

The present committee works extremely hard to raise funds for the hall, including a 200 club which has now been increased to a 280 club. Quizzes, casino nights, book sales, a square dance and race nights are among the functions organised by them and have helped to update the hall, including a toilet accessible by wheelchair users and a new kitchen.

The hall is currently used by many local clubs including sports groups, and young children's clubs and playgroups.

CHAPTER SIX

The Village Green

The village green has been the centre of village celebrations, fairs and fêtes throughout the years. The green was made up of three sections, the first being the triangle bounded by the Crossways hedge. This was enclosed by posts and a single iron rail, which all had to be painted every year – a white rail and purple brown posts. The path and ditch were well-tended, with a small white iron gate at each end of the railings. The path which runs along the side of Crossways was called the Holy Path and the trees on the green were known as Barclay's chestnuts.

The hedges surrounding the underground water supply tank installed in 1908 and the triangle of green on the right.

The second part of the green was where the Rev. Charles Barclay had the water fountain built in 1898 to mark the Diamond Jubilee of Queen Victoria. A cup hanging on a chain was provided to drink from, but unfortunately the fountain is no longer in use.

The third part of the green contained a large pond which attracted ducks and geese and where cows ate the grass and weeds, thus keeping the ponds clear. When grazing ceased, because of the milk marketing board's regulations, the ponds became murky with smelly muddy water. After a dry season when the water dried up, all the rubbish – old bottles, bicycle wheels, prams, bedsteads and a few drowned cats were exposed to public view (no rubbish collections in those days). The large pond was flanked by houses and Pretoria Cottages, now replaced by bungalows. In 1937 the ponds were filled in, due to misuse and because they had almost grown over.

Although the ponds are gone, there is still a path that runs across the centre of the green to remind us that it was once in three parts.

During the war, a large air raid shelter was built on the green, where the salt bin is situated today. Its entrance led underground to a chamber where there were bunk beds for the children and the elderly. When it rained the shelter unfortunately became flooded and also the pond leaked into it and became full of water, which led to the shelter collapsing and it became unfit for further use.

The green was also used by the ladies of the village to hang their washing on lines which were around the pond, and which stretched along the grass verges opposite the school and onwards to the top of Mount Pleasant. The women of the village were mostly washer women and took in washing from Haileybury College, Balls Park College, Brickendonbury, Stillmore's in Queen's Road and Christ's Hospital, the Bluecoats School in Hertford. The village was known locally as 'Soap Sud Island'. They all had there individual washing lines on the village green and fights would break out if someone used the line belonging to another. The washing was done in big tubs – first, scrubbing the cloths with grated soap, boiling in soda and then putting it through the mangle. School girls would collect the dirty washing on a Monday and return the clean washing back on a Friday, using wooden trucks with two handles. When the girls reached fourteen they were replaced with girls of about ten. Some of the carting was also done by Fred Cox, a contractor who lived in Crossways at the time which had grounds stretching down to the Townshend Arms. He and his wife, Rosetta, employed five women who worked in the old sheds in the garden and the washing was dried there, rather than on the green. He did much of the village's transporting with his many vehicles.

Crossways in 1966 when there were hedges surrounding it

A scene showing the washing lines in the distance on the grass verges, which form part of the Village Green.

The pond looking very clear and the water fountain to the left.

*The green in the present day with all traces of the pond
now a distant memory*

Recently Bob Frost, along with the help of some local men, built a Petanque pitch on the green for the game of French boules, which has been very popular with visitors as well as locals.

The green has also been used in recent years for bonfires on Guy Fawkes Night. The Parish Council organised a bonfire and fireworks for a couple of years, but an independent committee was formed in 2005, led by Richard Jacobs to resurrect this tradition. These have been a great success, with fantastic firework displays and great bonfires. Large crowds enjoy the occasion and support it by purchasing glow bands and flashing badges that light up the evening along with the fire and fireworks. Guys are provided by the village school children and extremely good they are too. The Parish Council has now been invited to take over the reins of the committee, with the same members organizing the event.

CHAPTER SEVEN

The Fields of Hertford Heath and what was built on them

The four fields pictured below in a map dated 1829, surrounded by Priors Wood, including the land just in front of them, have either been built on or have been acquired for recreation.

In the foreground Turnpike Road, now called London Road, is shown running from Haileybury College to Hertford. Also printed on the map (but not shown in this extract) was a list of the 'Headboroughs' on Hertford Heath allocated to those who were allowed to graze their horned cattle or horses on common ground and to collect three load of bushes. 'Lord John Townshend's Arms Public House' is shown at the bottom left of the map, with the 'Old Goat Public House' just above it. The map stated that the Manor of Great Amwell contained 104 acres, 2 rods and 0 poles unenclosed and 6 acres, 0 rods and 25 poles enclosed.

The four fields, described on the following pages, run from right to left.

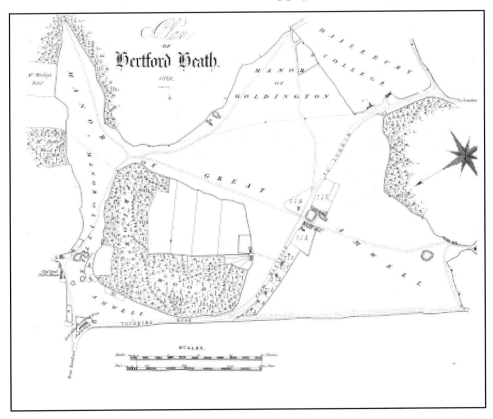

The First Field (from the right on the map)

The first field was called **Edgar's Ponds,** a name given to it by the locals because it was owned by Edgar Ernest George. Its previous owner was James Childs Jnr.

    The ground was made up largely of gravel pits which were full of water for most of the year, hence the name "Edgar's Ponds". Children would paddle in the shallow areas which could be hazardous with the possibility of broken bottles and other debris. "As a child, I had the misfortune to tread on a broken bottle in one of the ponds," the author recalls, "and had my first visit to a hospital to have the cut stitched." The ponds froze over during the winter which made for some precarious skating, and invariably children would arrive home with wet feet because the ice was thin and broke under their weight. There is a story of a boy that drowned in the deepest pond, and it was a very big dare if you skated on that one. Pictured below is the piggery that Edgar George used to keep at the top of the field.

    Edgar George was Racquets Coach and manager of the games shop at Haileybury from 1908-1920. He was also for many years chairman of Little Amwell Parish Council. He lived in a house called Oakdene in Mount Pleasant which is no longer there having been replaced by two bungalows. His field was sold to McMullen's of Hertford in 1950 and was subsequently sold on to James Albert Davies and others, for the development of Postwood Green which was completed in 1962.

The piggery which Edgar George kept at the top of the field.

Edgar George is on the left sitting on the fence outside Oakdene

Part of the Restrictive Covenants for the purchase of Edgar's field read as follows: *"In consideration of the premises the purchasers thereby jointly and severally covenanted with the Vendors that they the Purchasers and their successors in title would not carry on or permit to be carried on upon the said property thereby conveyed or part thereof the trade or business of an Innkeeper Victualler or seller of wines spirits porter stout ale or beer or any intoxicating liquors or mineral or aerated water is to be consumed either on or off the premises or a club where such liquors or waters were consumed distributed or sold".*

Part of Postwood Green used to be allotments. Gladys Jackson, the mother of John Cutler (formerly of Hertford Heath), is pictured sitting in the allotments, with Woodland Road houses in the background.

The Second Field on the Map

The Playing Field (Huson's/Lyne's) was formerly known as Barrow Wood Field and was part of Grimstead, Brimsdown and Priors Wood fields. It has had many owners, those documented in 1894 being William Gray, Joseph Chalmers Hunt, John Henry Grant and Arnold Havard Wright. Other names appear on the deeds from 1900 until it was sold by George Gray and Charles Gray Bullock for £500 to Mr. John William Huson in 1916. The four-acre field was used by Mr. Huson to keep a small dairy farm at the top of the field. Part of it was rented to the school at £7.10s per annum as a sports field for the school children.

It was later sold on to Mrs. Lyne who had riding stables at College Road Farm, which had also been owned by John Huson. Mrs. Lyne purchased the field for training her horses in.

In 1953 the Parish Council purchased the field from Mrs Lyne to provide a playing field for the local community. A Hertford Heath Playing Field Committee was formed to raise funds to help with the purchase, and people from the village worked for a number of years organizing events to help with the financing. Among those that worked very hard to negotiate the purchase were Fred Harrington, a district and parish councillor, and Lillian Bean, another village stalwart and long serving parish councillor. Support was also given by Haileybury College, with Mr. Ridsdill-Smith a member of the teaching staff doing much to help.

Children's swings a slide and a sandpit were supplied in the dip at the bottom of the field, and although this was the only playground equipment it was nevertheless appreciated by all village children. A tennis court was built on the opposite side of the field, but fell into disrepair and was pulled down to make way for the present children's playground. Football and cricket were played in the field and there used to be a cricket pavilion at the top of the field until the team was disbanded due to the development of housing on either side of the field.

The Playing Field and Children's Play Area today.

The Third Field on the Map

The Third Field (Lyne's) was also used for grazing cows and was later purchased by Mrs. Lyne. She eventually sold it along with the second field to the District Council for housing. This is now part of Trinity Road and Harrington Court, which was named after the late Councillor Fred Harrington.

The field was once used for hay making. This was great fun and was enjoyed by many of the local children. The local youths once had an old car in this field in which they took turns to learn to drive. During the evening it became somewhere to sit and chat, not something that would be allowed today.

The Fourth Field on the Map

The Fourth Field (Harvey's Field/Gifford's/Grimstead), now part of Trinity Road, is where the Belgic Burial was found.

This field has had three names throughout the years, the most recent one being "Harvey's Field", so called because Miss Harvey who owned the field had a house at the back of it. She had kennels and catteries where animals could be boarded, and if any of the local people had a problem with their cats or dogs she would give them help and advice. She was a member of the Our Dumb Friend League, an animal charity, and encouraged others to become members who were given badges with O.D.F.L. around the edges and a picture of a deer in the centre. Miss Harvey cared for a large number of animals and allowed well-behaved children into the cottage to see them. She would talk to them about the care of animals and give them an O.D.F.L. newsletter. Many years ago there was a grass tennis court at the top of the field. This field was sold to the District Council for housing by Miss Harvey.

Miss Harvey's house and Waterlily Pond in the Heath

Miss Harvey's house was located in Heath Lane close to Waterlily Pond in the Heath. The pond contained newts in the spring and used to stretch all the way down to the famous bumpy track used by children for riding their bikes, where a swing was attached to the bough of the old oak tree. This area now forms part of the Nature Reserve.

Priors Wood was formerly known as Grimstead Woods, a name originating from fossilised remains or ruins. Priors Wood dominated Hertford Heath in 1829 but its size decreased rapidly as the village grew with the building of more and more houses. Indeed the last remaining part was developed in 1975 to become Trinity Walk, Rushen Drive and later Oak Tree Close.

Priors Wood was a favourite playground for the local children from early days to the 1960's. It was a safe haven where games of make-pretend houses and pretend mums and dads were popular pastimes. Kiss-chase was also played and 'if you dare'. Holly Bush Hill was a memorable place in the woods, and the gravel pit sited at the far end of the wood is now the site of Rushen Drive.

A path that ran through it was used by children who lived in Woodland Road to go to school. Otherwise they used the "coke path" that ran from the island roundabout at the junction to Priors Close, then on to Church Hill. In those days there were only bushes where the most recent part of Woodland Road is now.

Part of Prior's Wood with Mount Pleasant in the background.

CHAPTER EIGHT

The Heath (Nature Reserve)

Adjacent to Priors Wood was the Heath, now a Nature Reserve, managed by the Herts & Middlesex Wildlife Trust. The Heath led to Much Wood, Leafy Oak Wood, Newgates Corner and then on to the Strawberry Fields. Picnics were held there in the summer where families picked the tiny but very tasty strawberries. The path then led on to the main road and across to Gypsy Lane. The College woods (Goldingtons or Goldings) was known as the Keepers and was fenced off from the Heath. Although this always has a no entry sign at the gate it was one of the local hunting grounds. Primroses used to grow in abundance there and the dam which has recently been repaired was used for sailing make shift boats, which inevitably sank after a very short time. The steep hill in front of the dam made for some serious tobogganing in the winter.

The Heath itself was enjoyed by everyone, as it is today, and we are very lucky to have it. However, there have been many changes over the years with the habitat diminishing over time. There used to be many hazelnut trees with heavy yields of nuts in September which were enjoyed by many. Blackberry bushes were more plentiful in the Heath, and far more bluebells and many more wildflowers grew there in the spring than they do today. Many more species of birds inhabited the heath, such as nightingales, linnets, nightjars, skylarks, turtle doves and many more cuckoos than today.

The Nature Reserve is in two parts separated by the B1197. Some excellent work has been done by the Herts & Middlesex Wildlife Trust, particularly to the ponds which have been dug out and enlarged. This has attracted ducks, and moorhens have nested and reared their young in them successfully for the past three years. The Heath is also the home of muntjac deer, rabbits and grey squirrels. The pond on the main path next to the fields was originally called the Railing Pond, as it used to have white posts and railings at the side of the path which led to Haileybury College, hence the name the College Path. The pond was so clear that it was sometimes used for swimming. The path was very well maintained and led down to the white gates. It was used by the men of the village who worked at the college, and they would light their way at night with a candle in a jam jar with string for handles.

In the days before dust lorries came to take away the rubbish, there was a section of land in the Heath called 'the Dungles' – it was used to dispose of old bottles, broken crockery, chamber pots, etc. This piece of land has been well sifted since then and some very interesting old bottles have been uncovered. Gypsies used to park their caravans in the Heath and would sell their wares of pegs, paper flowers etc: to neighbouring household's pegs. It was then a case of lock up your sheds as bikes would go missing?

One of the clearings in the Nature Reserve.

The main path that leads from Mount Pleasant to London Road and across to the Roundings, the second part of the Nature Reserve.

The Roundings, the second part of the reserve, is adjacent to Balls Woods and supports plants including common heather, purple moor grass, wavy hair grass, heath bedstraw and, in the summer, the small yellow flowers of tormentil (*potentilla erecta*) and petty whin (*genista anglica*) amongst other heathland species. Being a damp heath land there are a number of wet pools with sphagnum mosses and rushes which are a special habitat for dragon and damselflies. One of the ponds is home to a large number of great crested newts.

The woodland consists of mature hornbeam coppice and secondary oak and birch woodland. Commonly seen birds include the little owl, long-tailed tit, and nuthatch, tree creeper and lesser spotted woodpecker.

The Herts & Middlesex Wildlife Trust has a long-term management agreement with the owner, Haileybury College, and the reserve is designated a Site of Special Scientific Interest. See also colour photographs between pages 96 and 97.

Part of the Roman road, Ermine Street (left), the runs through the Roundings, and a sign (below) describes this. The Roman Road extends through the Roundings to Elbow Lane Farm, and then on to the Huntsman Pub in Goose Green. The pub was called the Green Man until the late 1900's. In the opposite direction it leads to the back of Hertford Heath Motors and on to London Road.

Clarice Pawsey wrote a poem about our woods, which was published in the Parish Magazine in September 1970.

In The Woods

One day I went a wandering
Through woods of leafy green
And 'neath the trees majestic
Bright blossoms could be seen.

The primrose and the bluebell
Anemone so white
Were lifting heads of beauty,
It was a wondrous sight.

The oaks and elms and sycamores,
The ash, the beech, the fir
All stood in glorious array
To make my sad heart stir.

Sweet notes the birds were rendering
In branches up above,
The finches and the thrushes
All sang their songs of love.

I roamed into a sunlit glade
Where tiny streamlets flowed
And there I sat and pondered
On what God had bestowed.

A rabbit and a squirrel
Drew nigh to comfort me,
And in the calm, clear water,
My reflection I could see.

With God's creation round me,
So peaceful and secure,
My strength, my faith, my courage
Came back again once more.

I walked from out that woodland,
My head held high in pride –
The Lord had spoken to me,
And he was at my side.

CHAPTER NINE

Shops, Farms, Businesses and Allotments

The village has only two shops at present, known locally as the Top Shop and the Bottom Shop, both in London Road. But less than sixty years ago there were all manner of shops – butcher's, baker's, electrical, farm, cobbler, hairdressing, fruit and vegetable, confectionery and grocery shops. Here is a brief account of most of them.

Shops in London Road

London Road is the main road that runs through Hertford Heath and in the early 20th Century the old Post Office was in the same vicinity as the present one. In 1924, it was just a little tarred cottage with Mr. William Ellis as the Postmaster in 1924. The row of cottages that stands at the side of the building used be called "The Old Post Office Cottages". Later the post office services were transferred to the top of London Road where the S.Z.I Food and Wine shop is now. At one time it was run two ladies, Ross and Barrett, and Brian Hawkins worked for them as the paper boy. Mr. and Mrs. Williams were the next proprietors who employed local lads for paper and grocery deliveries, among them John Cutler, John Anderton, Len Kiff and the three Phypers boys Ken, Derek and Ron. The round consisted of deliveries by bicycle with a large carrier on the front to London Road, Priors Wood Road, The Roundings, Haileybury College, Hailey Lane, Springle Lane, Ware Road, Hailey and Wollensbrook. For heavier loads and longer journeys Mr. Williams would take the boys in his Morris Minor van BJH 728.

John Cutler can remember one very strange women who would weigh all her groceries on her own scales, then check the bill – this often took ten to fifteen minutes; if any of the goods were a fraction under weight or if the bill was thought to be as little as a farthing more than she thought he had to walk back to the van and summon Mr. Williams to sort the problem out

He also employed three full-time staff at the shop, Miss Lucy Pile and Mrs Gladys Warren, with Miss Edwards at the Post Office counter. The shop was called simply The Post Office Stores, and later The Hertford Heath Stores.

Mr. Stevens took the shop over from Mr. Williams and the delivery boy for him was Bob Kimpton. It later changed hands again and was run for many years by George Kilminster as G & J Stores. He decided to dispense with the Post Office side of the business and it was transferred back to the same site as the original where Bill George's son, Robert, eventually inherited the shop. Bill George and his wife ran the shop as a grocery, greengrocery and sweet shop. For a period of time they had a café there where they served his homemade ice cream along with teas and snacks. Robert and his wife, Evelyn, ran the shop for many years and employed local people to deliver the mail, among them Lizzie Bottrell, Bob Sibley, Josie Cox, Edna Copeland and Jean Phypers. The sorting office was still in the back garden of the shop when Wendy Cousins, the latest owner, took over.

In Priorswood Road at the junction with London Road was the local barber's shop run by John Croft. In addition to hairdressing Mr. Croft worked as an undertaker and ran a football sweepstake at the shop.

In London Road, there was a butcher's shop opposite Old Forge Row that used to belong to Mr. John Pitt. There was an old slaughterhouse at the back of the garden which Mr. Pitt used for storage. Ken Cutler used to help him prepare the meat and would deliver it to customers in a horse and cart and later in a van. One of the delivery boys was Len Kiff, who used a bicycle with a basket on the front. On the odd occasion there would be a mishap and the bike would topple over and the meat would fall out of the basket. It was hit and miss if the orders were in the correct wrappers of newspaper when it eventually arrived at the customer's home. Previous proprietors were Miss Newman in 1902, in 1908 it changed hands to the Walker Brothers and in 1914 it was called W. George Frogley & Son. The next proprietors were Albert Woodrow and his two daughters until John Pitt took over. The last butcher to run the shop until it was converted back to a house was Mick Lee.

Next door was a small grocer's shop run by Mr. and Mrs. Jordan. Butter was weighed and wrapped in greaseproof paper and sugar was also weighed and put in blue bags. Mrs. Jordan had large jars of sweets to sell by the ounce.

Across the road, next to the Crown Public House (the Silver Fox), was the blacksmith's. Arthur Fletcher worked there for many years and for a period of time was also the licensee of the Crown. He had a son and two daughters. His son was a wheelwright and took over the business after his father's death, but business dwindled and he decided to close it down. Children would go there and ask to work the bellows and also to get their steel hoops repaired as they were always snapping. On the other side of the Crown was a wooden building where Mr. Rogerson ran a cobbler's shop. When he retired and the smithy closed, Frank Turner took over both buildings. He sold fruit and vegetables and used the old blacksmith's for garaging his delivery van and storing his goods. Frank delivered to customers at Hertford Heath, Hailey and Great Amwell.

At the other end of London Road, at the junction with Church Hill, was a grocery shop built in 1880 that was run by Miss Eliza French. She was called 'Smelly French' because she smelled everything before she sold it to her customers; even if she sold you shoe laces she smelt them first. In the 1901 census the premises is listed simply "The Shop". George Umney and his wife, Amy, took over from Miss French and ran the shop for many years. This is one of the shops where ration books were used by the locals during and after the Second World War. Mr. and

George and Amy Umney at their Ruby Wedding party.

Mrs Fewster took over the shop in 1960 and ten years later sold it to Mr. and Mrs Girling. The shop was then leased by them to Derek and Maureen Hodson and then for a short while to Margaret Collins. The lease was then transferred to Gerald and Rose Smart and they eventually purchased the property in 1987. In 1995 William and Christine Miles purchased the shop from the Smarts and later decided to lease the shop whilst continuing to live on the premises. Two local ladies, Diane Crosby and Julie Hann, leased the shop from 2004 to November 2007. Michelle, another local lady who used to serve in the shop, took over the lease from them and is currently running the shop as 'The Country Store'.

On the corner of Downfield Road was Watlings electrical and hardware store. This is one of the places where extremely heavy accumulators from the radio sets were taken to be recharged. Farther along from the Two Brewers Pub, Mrs. Hawkins ran a hairdresser's shop, in what was previously the Horse and Dray beer house. Next to that was a grocery and sweet shop run first by Mr. J. Adams, then by Mr. G. King, next was Mr. Brace, followed by Mr. Bowers and most recently by Mrs Bailey.

A short distance away on the other side of Downfield Road was the bakery. It belonged to the Chandler family and later Jaggs and Edwards. It was subsequently sold to Mr. Leslie Wren, who became famous for his bread and cakes; families' turkeys were sold and cooked there at Christmas time. Among those employed by him were Joe Bulley, Roy Kitching, Dick Fitzjohn, Fred Harrington and Sid Cox, with Mrs. Wren serving in the shop. Mr. Wren's brother Ernie had a bakery and two

Mr & Mrs Bob Gore standing in front of their car, outside their house. To the left of them is Bailey's shop.

The closure of the Hertford Heath bakery in 1972, and the old oven pictured when the building was being demolished.

shops in Hertford, one in Railway Street, the other in Ware Road.

The first house in Church Terrace next to the old school was a sweet shop, run in the late 19th century by William Hayden and later Daniel Hayden. Mr. Goldsmith was another proprietor followed by Mrs. Barnes and later still Mrs. Russell, who took over the shop and sold sweets from the front window to the school children. The shop is now a residential dwelling.

Milk Deliveries from the Farms

One of the milk deliveries was made by Frank Chapell's dairy of Bride's Farm in the Roundings. Frank was born in 1917 in South End, Stoneyhills, Hertfordshire. When he married his wife, Vera, he moved to London Road in Hertford Heath. In 1946 he worked for Arthur Martin of Bride's Farm and eventually took over the running of the dairy. He initially used a horse and cart later progressing to motorised milk floats. One of Frank's roundsmen was Sid Jackson. Later Frank together with his wife ran a toy shop in Bull Plain, Hertford, called The Hertford Toy Centre and another in Baldock Street, Ware named The Ware Toy Centre. In 1952 they moved to Rush Green and named the house they had built 'Pondcroft'.

Milk was also delivered by John Huson from College Road Farm, and Frank Potkins of Pondside Farm, Mount Pleasant. Another milk delivery man was Dick Cudmore who lived in Springle Lane, Hailey. He delivered milk by horse and cart and was a great character, always cheerful, and even in the worst of weather he would allow children to sit on the back of the cart to have a ride. Any horse manure was soon collected to put on the locals' rose gardens. In more recent years the Co-op was the main milk supplier.

Farms and Smallholdings

Amwell Place Farm in Downfield Road is reputed to be over 200 years old. The house has a Georgian front and a Victorian back extension. Inside the farm house

Frank Chappell's niece, Mavis, sitting on the milk float outside the Havelock Arms in London Road.

there used to be a ballroom which was not unusual in that era.

In 1875 John and Mary Blackley lived and farmed there, and in 1895 Mr. Henry Randall and Son lived and farmed there. It has been owned by a succession of people, among them Mr. Robert Hanbury in 1916 and Mr. Charles Augustus Christie in 1919. Although not occupying the farm house, Annie and Alfred Hayden rented and farmed the fields at the back of the property in 1916 and leased the land from Mr. Hanbury for £16.10s. a year. The size of the land was 14 acres, 3 rods and 16 poles. They lived at the top of Portland Terrace which had access to the fields from the back of the house. William Cooper was the next to manage the farm. When he retired, he had the house called 'The Downs' built just down the road.

The farm was sold to in 1923 to Hertfordshire County, who spilt it into four smallholdings for the heroes returning from the 1914-18 war. The four original holders were Tom Carter, Mr. Pawsey, Mr. Potkins and Eric Fitzjohn. Mr. and Mrs. Pawsey lived at the farm from 1923 until 1963. Clarice Pawsey's nick name for the house was "Old Bleakie"; they managed the dairy side of the farm and also kept pigs.

Peter Jollyman took over the dairy farming in 1963 from the Pawseys. He has since retired, but still lives in part of the farm house with his wife, Jo, and maintains the land at the back of the premises.

Jack Hayden was the son of Annie and Alfred Hayden. He managed a smallholding in Newgates Corner at the side of Much Wood. He raised two of his seven children in a small cottage on the farm. There is still a hard standing of concrete in the field which marks the spot on which the small house stood. Jack was also Pindar of the village for a period of time.

Apart from keeping cows, Frank Potkins' smallholding in Mount Pleasant had a shop that sold eggs and vegetables.

Amwell Place Farm and (right) Mr. and Mrs. Pawsey with Gerty Grunter the pig in 1929. Clarice Pawsey became the village's local poet (see Chapter 16).

Bride's Farm in the Roundings was one of the oldest farms on Hertford Heath, although it was situated in Great Amwell for many years until the parish boundary changes. It had been a farm since 1329 and had many owners, including its namesake, William Brydde.

In 1895 Mrs. Eliza Campbell is recorded as the farmer, with William Northern in 1902, and Mr. and Mrs. Apling in 1908. In more recent years it was farmed by Mr. Arthur Martin, as described on page 72. The farm is now used for riding stables and a Bed and Breakfast establishment.

Also in the Roundings was Elbow Lane Farm, at the end of the Roman road, first held by Richard Aldingbourne in 1250, whose name was corrupted to form 'Elbow' Lane. In later days it was run by George and Susie Shepherd. Susie was well known for serving teas, cakes and sandwiches in the farmhouse. Her 'Egg Teas', as she called them, were popular with villagers. They consisted of a boiled egg, toast or bread and butter, with jam trifle and a cup of tea. These were also popular with boys from Haileybury College, among them Stirling Moss, who later became a world class motor racing driver. On one occasion Stirling presented Susie with an oil lamp, this was among her most prized possessions and she proudly showed it to all her customers. But in 1946 there was a fire at the farm which was reputed to be caused by an oil lamp being knocked over and the building was badly damaged. Was this same lamp given to her as a present by Stirling? Who knows.? The farm is now used for equestrian training.

Other farms on and near the Heath were Huson's Farm near the College, Balls Park Farm, Jenningsbury, Foxholes and Rush Green farms. Rush Green Farm was also owned by the Hertfordshire Council; William Gray was the farmer in 1895 and William Thomas Cooper in 1901.

In the late 14th Century, John son of Robert Gamel held the land of 'Gameles' with its moated farmstead. The name lives on in Gamels Hall.

Businesses

Chandler's coal yard was located in Mount Pleasant and was sold to William and Stan Taylor after the coal strike of 1926. They eventually transferred the business to Rye House, Hoddesdon, but William and his wife continued to live in a small bungalow at the bottom of the site of the coal yard. William's son, Ron Taylor, inherited the business and continued to run it. He and his wife Maggie had a house built at the front of the old coal yard site which is still there today.

Mr. Harry Fitch was a builder on Hertford Heath as was his father before him. He carried on the business called H. Fitch & Son with his brother Bill. The building yard was in Mount Pleasant, and they built the three houses next to it which were eventually sold to Mr. Leslie Wren. They also repaired all the war damage to properties on the Heath. The sons were most famous for their building of the Village Hall in 1935.

William Gray had a large timber and builder's yard with steam saw mills in London Road. It stretched from the back of Heath Lane down towards the corner shop at the junction of Priors Wood Road and was a large source of employment in the village. He employed over a hundred men with the timber and brickworks. He used to buy from all over the south of England, sending out gangs of men to bring the timber home and stack it in large piles in the yard. Most of the blocks of old stock brick buildings in the village were built by William Gray in the late 1800's; they were built from bricks made in the brickfields in Hogsdell Lane, which was also owned by William Gray. He built the cottages at the start Downfield Road, those on Mount Pleasant between the Church and the Old School, and also the cottages to the right of the Top Shop in London Road. The last house to be built from these bricks was Crossways in Vicarage Causeway. The firm was put out of business by a disastrous fire in the early 1930's which destroyed everything in the builder's and timber yard. After the timber yard burnt down the land was taken over by Skylark Coaches. The buses went to Oxford Circus via Hertford and Ware every two hours from the College Arms.

Another source of employment for a dozen or so Heath men was at the Rope Factory in Gypsy Lane, Great Amwell. The men used to travel down through Leafy Oak on to Newgate's Corner, which had wooden gates across of which there are just two posts left, and on to the B1502. It used to be a wide road in those days and was used by horses and carts.

Garages

The local garage and car showroom in the centre of London Road at the Roman road junction was built on the site of the old police cottage and was owned by Reg Holman who operated a cycle shop there. Over time it evolved into a garage and was sold on to Bob Breckon, who employed among others Ron Childs and Derek Phypers. Eddie Smith was the next owner who eventually passed the business on to his son Mike and the garage is now called Hertford Heath Motors. Mike's son Andrew is now in partnership with his father.

Another garage, Haileybury Motor Works, is situated in College Road. It was once owned by Mr. Maynard and, in addition to selling and servicing cars, they also recharged accumulators used on radio sets, as did Hertford Heath Motors and Watlings Electrical shop.

Chimney Sweeps

The chimney sweep would call every four to five weeks. This was necessary because of the amount of wood burned on fires and the amount of soot it generated. One of the local chimney sweeps was Mr. Camp who lived in Mount Pleasant. He walked round the village with his brushes, rods and other equipment. The soot from the chimneys was kept for the gardens. Wood could be obtained from Mr. Bert Vousden from Priors Wood Road. He delivered bags to people in the village for a very modest price. Jack Webb and his two brothers, Butty and Joe, who were born in The Street, were also chimney sweeps in the village.

Village Policemen

We used to have our own dedicated policeman who lived in the village police house. Among the officers were PC Trussell, PC Winters, PC MacLean, PC Smith, PC Pearman, PC Albert Cooke, PC Percy Richards and PC Don Street.

They kept keep law and order in the traditional way; offending youths were cautioned and given a stern telling off, and this was usually enough. Don Street in particular will be remembered for his fair but friendly and cheery nature. The police house he lived in was in London Road, but is now a private dwelling. Other police houses used before that were one on Church Hill and one on the site of the local garage in London Road.

Allotments

Apart from the allotments in London Road, there have been others in the not so distant past. One at the rear of the Village Hall adjoined Woodland Road on land owned by Haileybury College, and was also used for keeping poultry. Another was in Mount Pleasant, backing on to part of Rushen Drive. Yet another was behind Hillcrest Cottages in Downfield Road stretching for some distance either side of them.

Allotment judging in Downfield Road

Part of the London Road allotments has been developed into a wildlife meadow with a large pond, which should encourage a variety of wild flowers to flourish and provide a natural habitat for birds and insects. The most recent venture was the opening of Bob's Pond, named after Bob Akers, the allotment manager, pictured above at the opening of the pond.

*Some advertisements for local shops and businesses
in the Parish Magazine, 1939*

CHAPTER TEN

Fêtes, Fairs and Celebrations

As in most villages, fêtes have been held in Hertford Heath in variousplaces throughout the years, the first being in the Kissing Gates Field on London Road close to the Townshend Arms.

A picture taken by the Hertfordshire Mercury in the 1950's of a fête organised by the Hertford Heath Playing Fields Committee. More than £33 was raised on the day for the general fund of the playing field.

Fêtes were held in the field owned by Mrs. Lyne at the back of Woodland Road to raise money for the purchase of the site, for the community to use as a playing field. These continued after the purchase to raise more funds for the improvement of the playing field, one of which was the tennis court pictured in the background of this picture. Among the people watching are Pat, Eileen and May Porter, Cecil Aldridge, Ken Kitchen with son Malcolm, Jimmy Johnson and daughter Christine, Bobby Akers, Bob Spurgeon with son Robert, and Bill Hayden. Emmy Harwood and Doris Spurgeon are playing bowls.

Many locals will remember the annual church fêtes which were held in the old Vicarage gardens. It was referred to as the Vicarage Garden Party, and events included a Bonny Baby Contest, Lucky Dip, homemade cakes for sale, fancy dress competitions, and stalls set up by local residents. In the evening there would be dancing on the lawns with music provided by a gramophone and sometimes a piano.

All the fun of the fair at this fête in Kissing Gate Field in 1921 –
and athletics too! in 1921

The Women's Institute would also put on short plays.

Fêtes were also held in the gardens of Major and Mrs Denny's home, the White House in London Road. The Village School has always held annual fêtes in the summer, a tradition that continues to this day. Fêtes were held at the old peoples home called Heathfield that was on site of Old Forge Row along London Road. One of the fêtes in 1977 was opened by the Mayoress of Hertford, Mrs Checkley, and Mrs Crossgrove of Heathfield was the organizer. The Over-60 Club helped to make the afternoon a success. Heathfield was built on the site of an old country house owned by Major Cronin which had a large orchard at the rear. When it was decided to close Heathfield, a film company used the building for the making of the film *A Bridge too Far*. This was an exciting time in the village and was watched by neighbours with interest.

Villagers enjoying one of the fêtes, with Mrs Doris Bulley and Mrs Lillian
Bean from the over 60's club manning one of the stalls.

Two scarecrows from the W.I. fête in 2005.

The most recent fêtes have been held on the Village Green. A fête committee was formed and with a lot of hard work by local volunteers, they have been very successful for many years. Local organisations and groups surround the green while events take place in the central arena. Bowling for the pig used to be a traditional event, but more recently pet shows and tug-of-war have featured.

The fête committee disbanded for a few years, but in 2005 the Women's Institute put on a fête with a scarecrow theme. Villagers were encouraged to make scarecrows and put them in their front gardens with a prize given for the best entry. In 2006 a new committee was formed and the fete was resumed much to the delight of the village people. It was decided to have the fete during July, instead of the August Bank Holiday weekend as in the past. The fête was a huge success and was held again in 2007 with a great deal of work put in by the committee, headed by Alan Howard and Brenda Wilson. Hopefully the tradition of an annual fête will continue for the foreseeable future. See also colour photographs between pages 96 and 97.

The balloon race at the 2006 fête, held to raise funds for the fireworks display later in the year; and (right) the tug-of-war was still going strong in 2006.

Fairs on the Village Green

There used to be an annual fair on the Village Green during the month of June. The caravans of Manning's arrived every year and the fairground workers set up Swing Boats, the Waltzer, a Carousel, Bumper Cars, Tunnel-of-Love, Coconut Shies, the Rifle Range, even a barrel organ and numerous other stalls – and of course candy floss for the children. At one of the fairs, there was a very strange attraction which comprised a badger in a cage from which a stick protruded – people were encouraged to wiggle the stick and the badger would bite it. But that was a one-off thankfully. The occasional incident occurred at the fair – fortunately only rarely – such as when Norman Childs, a local man, fell out of the swing boats and broke two ribs.

The loud music played by Manning's became too much for some residents that lived close to the green and it was decided to discontinue the fair in the late 1950's

Prior to the fairs on the Village Green there was some held on the Heath at the end of Mount Pleasant.

Celebrations Throughout the Years

Throughout the years, Hertford Heath has celebrated special occasions in a big way, especially coronations and royal jubilees. Beacons of between 20 and 30ft high, with huge constructions of wood and metal, were lit on the field behind Amwell Place Farm, known as Beacon Field. Among them were two for Queen Victoria's Golden Jubilee in 1887 and Diamond Jubilee in 1897, and others for King George V's coronation in 1910.

On May 6th 1935, King George V's Silver Jubilee was celebrated with the village putting on a spectacular programme of events including:

10.30 am: there was an official thanksgiving service with a short address by the Master of Haileybury, the Rev. E.F. Bonhote.

11.30 am: the broadcast of a service from St. Paul's Cathedral was heard on a radiogram, kindly lent by Mr.L.G. Bland of Hertford.

2.00 pm: there was a Parade and Procession of decorated private cars, trade motor vehicles, trade horse-drawn vehicles, and motor cycles, gathered in front of te Goat Inn. Pedal cycles parked at the front of the school, perambulators, push carts, sugar boxes, and anything else on wheels assembled inside the school playground. Red, white and blue rosettes were handed out to the first three winners in each event.

3.00 pm: sports in the School Football Field, where children under five years of age were given Jubilee Mugs and sweets after the sports events.

5.00 pm: tea for all school children in the Village Hall.

6.30 pm: the day progressed with a Comic Football Match on the School Field with Mr. Hayden's XI v. Mr. Croft's XI.

8.00 pm: broadcast of the speech by His Majesty the King was heard in the Village Hall.

10.00 pm: rocket firing and lighting of the official Beacon on the Village Football Ground, and the proceedings ended with the singing of the National Anthem.

Some of the villagers in fancy dress and celebrations on the Village Green.

The Silver Jubilee beacon on the Village Football Ground (Carter's Field in Downfield Road). Among the men pictured here are: Mr. Phypers, Mr. Todd, Harry Turville, Mr. Camp, Charlie Lee, Mr. Penn and Mr. Wilson.

Left: the Silver Jubilee beacon at its full height. Right: a smaller beacon on Carter's Field for the Coronation of King George VI on 12th May 1937.

Part of the 1937 Coronation parade in London Road.

Celebrations for V.E. Day (Victory in Europe) saw many street parties, with this one being held in the Roundings on August 30th 1945.

The Coronation of Queen Elizabeth II on 2nd June 1953 was the first coronation to be televised and many watched the crowning in their own homes. However, the village still held a carnival and fancy dress parade which was hastily transferred to the Village Hall for the judging, because of the very heavy rain which caused some of the outfits to become very bedraggled by the time they reached the hall. The winner of the children's section was John Harwood dressed aptly as a television set.

The Kimpton boys, Bob and Colin, dressed as Pirates ready for the Parade, and (right) Frank Turner dressed as a Sheik in the Parade along Mount Pleasant.

This programme for the 1953 Coronation was issued to all the community.

Hertford Heath celebrated in style for the Silver Jubilee of Queen Elizabeth II on 7th June 1977. The programme of events started with a Gymkhana in Chappell's Field, Downfield Road, followed by bicycle events, proficiency tests and treasure hunts beginning from the school playground. Events on the Village Green in the afternoon included a parade of 1950 vintage cars, a fancy dress parade including decorated dolls prams, bicycles and go-carts, folk dancers, children's sports, pubs sports 'It's a Knockout' and finally a pet show. There were various stalls on the green selling food and drink, a beer tent run by the Townshend Arms, slide and swing boats, a crèche for toddlers, a dunking machine, jubilee mugs for sale, and a balloon stall. The evening activities included a pig roast and dancing to a four piece band until midnight. Many street parties were held with the one below being in Woodland Road.

CHAPTER ELEVEN

Football and Cricket in Hertford Heath

Hertford Heath Football Club is recorded in existence as long ago as 1896. Various teams were formed, among them the Hertford Heath Football Team and the Hertford Heath Recreational Club.

In December 1896 Hertford Heath's 2nd team played Stanstead Abbots 2nd team resulting in a 0 – 0 draw. In Jan 1897 Hertford Heath played Rye Park Continuation team losing by 2 goals to 1. Heath's Team consisted of A. Hayden, H Chessell, Foster, Pavey, Bryant, W Judd, C Porter, H Gray, Lyons, W Fitch, and J Howe.

The H.H. Recreational Club played a game in November 1897 against Hertford Grammar School. The team comprised: Allen, Nottage, Bennett, Lyons, Howe, Judd, Mardell, Rudd, Fitch, Bryant, and Gray.

In December 1897 Hertford Heath drew with Horns 0 – 0. Heath's Team: Randall, Bennett, Chessell, Lyne, Nottage, Howe, Judd, Bulley, Rudd, and Matthews.

Hertford Heath joined the East Herts District League Division II mid-way through the 1897/98 season losing their first match against Chantry Villa (Bishops Stortford) by 1 – 0. The first full season in the league was 1898/99.

The most successful year was 1901, when the Hertford Heath team, playing in the East Herts League, played 14, won 13, and lost 1, goals for 56, against 12. The team's ambition to win the cup was unsuccessful, losing the last game to Rye Park resulting in the cup being held jointly.

In 1907-08 a team known as 'Little Amwell' was affiliated to the Hertfordshire Football Association. Miss Vera Barclay, the daughter of the vicar, Charles Barclay, organised the team; Vera was the driving force behind the administration of that early team and her sister, Ursula Barclay, was the secretary. In those days the team had its headquarters in The Goat public house, and played on Carter's Field at Amwell Place Farm. It is rumoured that to help inspire these noble gentlemen on a Saturday afternoon, they were allowed one free half-pint of beer before they took to the field.

This medal dated 1902-3 was found by Mick Gannon in the Long Meadow, London Road, while metal detecting.

The team in 1909 – among the players pictured here are
George Frederick Cox and Jim (Whiffler) Phypers.

With the coming of the the First World War, the club like many others in the area folded, but came together again in 1918 with an inaugural meeting in the Two Brewers public house in The Street (now Downfield Road). The club moved its head-quarters to the School Cottage and joined the Hertford and District Junior League, running two teams. The team, which included Cecil Childs, Fred Plum, Tom Hudson and their workmanlike captain Fred Pratt, won its first trophy in the memorable season of 1924-5. The 1st XI were Division I champions, and the reserves finished top of Division II, thus becoming the first club in the league to win the "double."

Shortly after becoming champions again in 1931-2, Hertford Heath left the Hertford and District League to play in the East Herts League where they played until 1939.

During that period they finished runners-up once and were beaten by semi-finalists in the Herts Junior Cup, but honours eluded them until after the Second World War.

Football in the 1930's was tough. The club had almost 50 players on its books, and none would stand any nonsense if they suspected unfair play. One tale is of a referee who came from the same village as the Heath's opponents. The team was unhappy about some of his decisions and after the match was he unceremoniously dumped in a pond on the village green.

There is another story about one particular game when things got a bit rough. After the final whistle one of the players in the picture on page 89, Joe Webb, who

Hertford Heath 1931-32.
Back row (left to right): J. Howsen (treasurer), H. Anderton, H. Farnham,
G. Camp, W. Jordan, H. Judd, J. Webb, C. Todd, (chairman)
Front row: J. Phypers, F. Farnham, H. Dickenson, H. Akers, J. Potkins.

at that time was the Area Light Heavyweight Boxing champion and used to box at the Hertford Corn Exchange, challenged the members of the opposite side that he would take them on one at a time, but there were no takers!.

Both Bob Akers' father and mother were involved with the football club at this time, she used to make home-made ginger wine for the players, which they would drink at half time, and a story got around that the Hertford Heath players were boozing in the interval.

Opposition was tough in those days with Allen and Hanbury's, and the Territorial Army from Ware (Terriers) being some of the toughest opponents. Cries of "Come on the Bush" could be heard from the supporters to encourage the Hertford Heath team on.

After the Second World War, Hertford Heath joined the Hertford and District League, running two teams. Their first success came in 1954-5 when they finished on top of Division I. Their best-known players at that time were Norman Childs, George Watson, Horace (Podge) Hornett, Stan Smith, Bob Spurgeon, Gordon Ward, Ron Barwick, Peter Childs and Bob Akers. A highlight for the team in 1961-2 the club did another "double," winning the Divisions I Championship and the Challenge Cup.

For many years the team had been aided financially by their supporters, who contributed to a box that was passed around the ground on match days. During

The winning team of 1961-2 with the Championship and Challenge cups.

Back row (left to right): *Alf Foster, Bill Akers, Peter Childs, Alan Davies, Bob Kimpton, Derek Akers, Alec Anderton, Stan Bean, Bill Darnell, Tuck Angus and Malcolm Pavey.* Centre row: *John Harwood, Gavin Angus, Denny Adams, Bob Burns, Mick Rolfe, Jim Davis and Derek Thompson.* Front row: *Malcolm Newton and Bob Akers.*

1934. the sum of £4.13s. 0d. was collected from the supporters of which £4. 3s. 6d. was spent on the referee's fees. One referee even forced the club to pay a 2s.6d repair bill after one player trod on his watch!

Hertford Heath have played on four different pitches – after the Kissing Gate Field opposite the War Memorial, Carter's Field the back of Amwell Place Farm and the Long Meadow along London Road, they transferred to the pitch on the playing field in Trinity Road and have stayed there ever since.

The team was playing in the Herts Senior County League Division One in the year 2005/6. The pitch on the playing field has been upgraded to allow the team to enter the Herts Senior County League Premier Division 2006/7; railings have been erected around the pitch with hard standing for spectators.

The programme for the Hertford and District Football League Challenge Cup Competition 1961-1962

DIVISION 1

CHALLENGE CUP FINAL

1961-1962

HERTFORD HEATH

v

N A Z E I N G

*   *   *

Easter Monday 23rd April 1962

Hoddesdon Town F. C. ground

Kick off . 3.0 p.m
(Extra time if necessary)

Good afternoon,

Today's match brings together two teams who have not previously met in any of the League's Challenge Cup finals and we offer a welcome and congratulations to both Hertford Heath and Nazeing on reaching this stage of the Division 1 competition.

It is also the first time for many years that a final has been played in the Hoddesdon area, and the Executive Committee expresses its thanks to the Hoddesdon Town Football and Cricket Clubs for so kindly allowing this delightful ground and other facilities to be placed at the disposal of the League this afternoon.

After a lapse of several years, HERTFORD HEATH re-entered the League last year. This season, they have repeated their success of seven years ago by winning the Division 1 League championship. They have never before reached the final of the Challenge Cup.

The same cannot be said of NAZEING, formerly a Premier division side - for it was in that sphere that they twice carried off the Challenge Cup - the last occasion some eight years ago when they beat near neighbours Roydon at Hoddesdon arena. It is, however, their first appearance in the Division 1 final.

HERTFORD HEATH

R.

(White)

L.

R. KIMPTON

A. DAVIES   A. ANDERTON

J. DAVIS   R. BURNS   R. AKERS

M. NEWTON   G. ANGUS   D. ADAMS   M. ROLFE   J. HARWOOD

O

H. BODEN   J. NETTLE   I. MOFFATT   J. LEGGETT   R. NETTLE

F. WILKINSON   J. GODFREY   D. DODD

E. ELLIOTT   A. WELCH

A. PAYNTER

L.

N A Z E I N G

R.

(Red & Green)

Referee : Mr. L. Sinkins (Cheshunt)

The Football Dinner and Dance, May 1954,
in the Mayflower, Hotel Hertford

Among those present were:
  Standing at the back: George Watson;
  Right-hand table: Violet and Doug Newton, Maggie and Cecil Aldridge,
  Bob and Joyce Akers, Amy and Jack Webb, Albert Turville, Sis and Jack
  Anderton, Norman Childs, Jock Heaps, Lou King, Denny Wilcher, and Sylvia
  and Stan Smith.
  Left-hand table: Bob Sibley, Derek Akers, Ron Turville, Cyril Turville, Eric
  and Edna Lewis, and Podge Hornett.

Cricket

Hertford Heath has a long history of playing cricket with records showing that the team held meetings in the Village Hall between 1935 and 1937. The team was revived between the years 1948 to 1964, playing in Pawsey's Field, on the other side of Downfield Road from where football was played in Carter's Field. Later it transferred to the Long Meadow, and then the playing field. They had fixtures against other villages, Haileybury College and the Goat public house.

The Cricket Team playing in Pawsey's field, Downfield Road in 1951
Top Row: Chairman Mr. Ridsdill-Smith, Bob Sibley, Ted Childs, Michael Hunt,
Bill Hayden, Harold Copeland, Ernie Cox, Jimmy Johnson.
Front Row: Stan Bean, Jack Penn, Bob Akers, John Brown and Ken Phypers.

Most players came from the village with some from Haileybury College. Boys of senior school age were also eligible to join the club; among them were John Dickinson, John Cutler and Brian Umney. The club colours were maroon and blue. In 1954 the annual subscription for playing members was 5s. for under 16 years, 10s. for age 16 to 18 years, and 20s. for the over 18's.

The team had many capable players. Captains included Ernie Cox and Bob Akers, who also kept wicket. Bowling was led by Harold Copeland and Gordon Graves, batsmen included Fred Bush who scored a century in one afternoon and Ted Childs, who achieved the same in one hour! Support was provided by R.O. Sibley, as club scorer; his son Bob Sibley also played for the team. James (Jock) Heeps was the umpire, a role also undertaken occasionally by Bill Hayden when not playing in the team. Players' wives provided tea, sandwiches and cakes at the interval in home matches.

The team playing on the long meadow pitch London Road with the Balls Park Teachers Training School all girls team in 1952. Some of the Hertford Heath team members are: Tony Drury, Ted Childs, Captain Bob Akers, Michael Fox, Harold Copeland, Bob Sibley, Jack Penn, Stan Bean, Claude Camp, Michael Hunt and John Cutler.

The cricket team in the later years when the pitch was on the playing field. Left to right: Jimmy Johnson, Bob Akers, Ted Childs, Bob Sibley, Fred Bush, Teddy McBean, Jack Penn, Stan Bean, Ernie Cox, Jimmy Brace, Jock Heaps, Charlie Chapman. Umpire R.O. Sibley. The young girl on the left is Christine Johnson age 3, Jimmy Johnson's daughter.

A pavilion was built at the top of the playing field shortly after this letter was sent to club members in April 1954.

HERTFORD HEATH CRICKET CLUB

President – A.F. MacCallan Esq., C.B.E., F.R.C.S.
Chairman – G. Ridsdill-Smith, Esq., T.D., M.A.
Hon. Treasurer – E. Cox, Esq., Upper London Road, Hertford Heath.

27th April 1954

Dear Club member,

The cricket season is with us again and I have pleasure in forwarding you the fixture list for this year. I am sure you will agree that Jack Penn has done a good job and our thanks are due to him for his efforts.

Also enclosed are the Club's revised rules which no doubt you will read at your leisure particularly the paragraph concerning subscriptions.
Ernie Cox will be delighted to write out your receipt.

You will probably be aware that a new cricket table has been laid for our use by the Parish Council and a few of our members have recently been rolling and cutting it. The dry spell has not helped the table but it has settled down fairly well. As a temporary measure Bill Hayden and Bobby Akers have offered to act as groundsmen but your help is sought through out the season to keep the ground in as good a condition as possible. As soon as the evenings become a little longer we expect to resume out Tuesday and Friday evenings meetings at the ground to do any work required on the pitch and for practice. Will you make an effort to come along next Friday the 30th April, about 7.30 pm so that a start can be made and also for the purpose of arranging teams for the weekend match. Our Saturday away game of course clashes with the Cup Final but we must do our best to honour the fixture.

There is little likelihood that the pavilion will be delivered for our first game unfortunately. The delay has been most disappointing but your committee is determined that we will have a building shortly. There is no reason to suppose that it will not be the one we have ordered but if delivery cannot be obtained within the next two or three weeks other arrangements must be made.

In conclusion I should like to say on behalf of the committee that we are relying on your continued support for this season. We are hoping that this year will be our most successful one but so much does depend on your efforts.
Please canvass the club amongst your friends and endeavour to obtain new members.

Kind regards,

Yours sincerely,
W.D.TOWNSEND, Hon. Sec.
(43, Charmouth Road, St Albans)

Reluctantly the cricket team had to disband at the end of the 1964 season, as it had become impossible to play safely due to housing developments on both sides of the playing field.

CHAPTER TWELVE

Clubs and Societies

Over the years many clubs have been formed in the village catering for a wide range of age groups and interests, some are still running whilst others have disbanded.

The Youth Club

In 1935 an informal Youth Club was formed by a few boys, aged twelve to thirteen, and held in a shed at the back of Bobby Akers' parents' house in Jesmond Cottages. The group included Bobby Akers, Jeff Brown and Bob Beadle. They read books among other activities restricted by the size of the shed. The group were recognised as a Youth Club after a few months.

The first official Youth Club was formed in 1950, originally called the Hertford Heath Labour League of Youth. It changed its name to the Hertford Heath Youth Club to remove the obligation for members to join the Labour Party before being permitted to attend. Many village people have volunteered their help over the years to keep the club running. It has been held in the Village Hall and for a period of time in the Village School, before reverting back to the Village Hall until sadly it closed in 2003. Among the Youth Club leaders were: Mr. Kanolty, David Smart, Gary Hayes, Joyce Wright, Victor Penny, Sid and Annie Pavey, Ken Smith, Peter Risk, Pam Kimpton, Katherine Newton and Linda Barley.

Joyce Wright was Youth Club leader from 1962-1972. She came to the village in 1960 and wanting to help the community took over the running of the older boys' club for some time on her own. Help did eventually arrive with Cecil Aldridge from Woodland Road instructing the boys in woodwork activities. Midnight walks were very popular events organised by Joyce. Later, Victor Penny from Hoddesdon offered his help to form a five-aside-football team which was very successful in the South of England League. Victor succeeded Joyce when she retired.

Many people have helped the leaders to run the Youth Club – to mention just a few Fred Harrington, Jim Locking, Mrs. Tomsett, and in later years Gloria Pead, Lorna Clapp and Margaret Gannon. During the time of Pam Kimpton, Katherine Newton and Linda Barley's leadership the mixed children's Youth Club came under the care of Hertford Regional College at Ware and leaders were sent there for training. The club ran two sessions on a Friday evening, with 7–10 year olds for the first hour and a half, followed by the 11–16 year olds for the later part of the evening. Activities included obstacle races and games for the younger children, with snooker, pool tables, indoor football and badminton for the older ones. Outings to the Zoo

A photograph of Hertford Heath Chapel, taken by Mrs. Margaret Porter a few days before it was demolished in 1996 (see pages 25-26). The dog belonged to Mrs. Porter.

Holy Trinity Church during the Queen's Silver Jubilee celebrations in 1977.

This very old oak is adjacent to the bumpy track through the Nature Reserve (see Chapter 8) and looks majestic when in full leaf in Spring. The branches have often been used for swings.
Below: a mallard family on the Railing Pond in 2005.

Scenes from the fête on the Village Green:

Above: the Village Hall Committee at their bric-a-brac stall in 1997, when the theme was Chinese style. Left to right: Pam Kimpton, Katherine Newton, Violet Newton and Ruth Webb were dressed to impress.

Below: Brian Bishop and Bob Akers manning the Horticultural Society stall.

Above: the Goat public house in 1998 (see page 114).
Centre: a November Fifth bonfire on the Village Green.
Bottom: some of the Guys made for the occasion.

and Thorpe Park were among the most popular trips enjoyed by the children. At the annual Village Fête, the Youth Club would have a tombola stall to raise funds for these trips and another fund raiser was the occasional jumble sale held in the Village Hall.

Linda Barley was the last Youth Club leader in the village until her retirement, and sadly there has not been a Youth Club since then. In 1978 the Youth Club entered a float in the Hertford Carnival with the theme being Wurzel Gummidge with one or two Aunt Sallys.

The competitors on the float were: back row left to right: Lisa Finch, Adrian Race, Simon Kimpton, Jason Phypers, James Gannon, Kim Barley and Michael Race. Front row: Gary Barley, Rickie Pead, Amanda Risk, Debbie Pead and Tina Jones.

Left: Katherine Newton, Diane Burton, Linda Barley and Betty Collins at one of the village fêtes. Right: Linda's husband Stuart helping as driver of the float at the Hertford Carnival.

The Women's Institute

The Women's Institute is a long lasting society, which has been very successful in years gone by and still going strong today. Members are involved in providing teas and cakes at all the fêtes and many functions in the Village Hall. The meetings are currently held in the Mission Room, but have also been held in the Village Hall and the old school building.

Some W.I Minutes from 1918 to 1945

On 19th November 1918 it was decided to start a Women's Institute in Hertford Heath. The Hon. Mrs Gibbs was in the Chair, Speaker Mrs Warner. The following were elected as members of a committee:

> Mrs Florence Barclay, Mrs Malim, Mrs Tennant, Mrs Ehrthe, Mrs Milford, Mrs Nottage, Mrs Bulley, Miss Chessell, Miss A Barclay, Misses George, Mrs Ellis and Mrs Huson.

The committee proceeded to elect the following officers of the Institute:

Mrs Florence Barclay	President
Mrs Malim	Vice President
Mrs Tennant	Hon. Treasurer
Mrs Huson	Secretary

The meeting was held in the Mission Room and the next meeting for Tuesday November 26th was to be held at Ravenscroft.

In 1921 a resolution was passed and considered for the amalgamation of the National Institute of Women's Institute and the National Institute of Lands Women. This was to raise awareness for the need of country to raise its own crops due to the shortage brought about by the First World War. Women were encouraged to do their best help with the crisis by instigating the use of allotments to grow vegetables for this purpose.

In 1926 the Mission Room was provided with electric which the secretary at that time described as "a great addition to the brightness and cheerfulness of its appearance".

The meetings were transferred to the new Village Hall in May 1935, and 50 members were present.

1937 saw a roll call for suggestions to beautify the village in celebration of the Coronation of King George VI. It resulted in some useful and original ideas, amongst them being (1) the acquisition of the piece of waste land opposite the College Arms with the view to clearing the site, supplying seats and if necessary planting trees. (2) The erection of a bus shelter by the Townshend Arms. (3) Improvement of the pond on the Heath, planting of trees, and penalizing the throwing of tins into the pond. (4) More lighting in the village and surroundings. (5) Better paths and (6) the building of new schools.

In 1939 normal monthly meetings were put on hold owing to the outbreak of war and all meetings and arrangements were cancelled. Meetings were resumed in 1940 with a demonstration on wartime cookery and how to grow more vegetables to help with the food shortage. Parcels organised by the W.I were also sent to the troops. The Secretary's report for 1945 noted the joy and thankfulness for the end of the war, and with peace came thoughts of running homes with the utmost efficiency.

A group photograph of the Women's Institute in 1960 taken in Gamels garden. Back row from left to right: Miss Huson, Kay Turton, Vera Mead, Esme Nix, Betty Boote, Brenda Wilson, Nancy Jordan, Mary Denny, Rene Camp and Freda Abrahams. Second row: Doreen Foster, Edna Lewis, Mrs Bearder, Mrs Crofton, Mrs Ashley, Jean Dorken, Joyce Akers, Janet Langman, ? ? Mrs Pearman, ? ? Front row: ? ? Elsie Randall, Mrs Fewster, Clarice Pawsey, Mrs Spencer visitor from Australia, Mrs Wilson, Mr. Spencer, Caroline Cox (Secretary), Mrs Baker and Mrs Bunce.

The club celebrated its 600th meeting on 2nd February 1977 with Joyce Akers baking a special cake for the 60th anniversary of the club. Mrs Esme Nix was the President and the speaker for the evening was Joan Lash who talked about "Elephants, Earthquakes and Executives".

The 800th meeting was in November 1995, a sad time with the illness of Daphne Brown, a much loved member, who sadly died in 1998. The club has run successfully throughout the years with many varied and interesting meetings, Pat Webster is currently its President and Beryl Dymock the secretary. Joyce Akers has

The W.I. put on a fashion show in the village hall, with dresses from Maison-Ellen of Ware in July 21st 1977. Ladies modelling the dresses at the Village Hall are: Kim Reynolds, Christine Francis, Jo Jollyman, Sheila Burr, Muriel Burr, Mrs Skeels, Margaret Sharpe, ? and Belinda and Jackie Brown.

been the longest serving member of the W.I. joining in 1948, but she sadly died in 2007.

The Ladies Circle

Another long standing club is the Ladies Circle which evolved from the Mothers' Union. When first formed it was mistakenly thought that only women who had children

The Ladies Circle in 1966 pictured in the Vicarage gardens with the Rev. John Budd and his wife, Jill.

could attend. Its name as the Mothers' Union was changed in the 1950's to enable all women to attend. Kath Childs is currently the Leader.

The Royal British Legion

The Royal British Legion Women's Section had a branch in Hertford Heath for many years with Olive Davison as its last President. It disbanded in 1998. Lily Bean was a former President with Eva Hart, May Sheppard and Elsie Johns three of its secretaries. Other members have been Mrs. Smart, Mavis Chappell, Stella Partridge and Joyce Carter. Stella and her sister Joyce trained as the banner carriers. Meetings were held in Beacon Court and the Mission Room. During the 1940's there was also a small branch of a British Legion Men's Section, which lasted for just a few years but disbanded as they did not have enough to do.

The Trinity Club

Another successful club is the Trinity Club which has been meeting for a number of years now with Jean Bawcutt at the helm. This is a light-hearted small group of ladies who meet once a month with a varied programme of crafts, demonstrations and speakers. There is no committee just a friendly membership.

The Hertford Heath Horticultural Society

The Hertford Heath Horticultural Society has been in existence for many years with the present secretary, Fiona Castle, ably taking over from Brian Bishop after his death. The annual horticultural show is still being held in the Village Hall, but with not quite the same number of entries as there used to be, but is still popular with gardeners and allotment holders.

The Horticultural Society Annual Show in 2007 Bob Akers presiding, with Jean Bawcutt presenting the prizes. Kath Childs won an amazing eight firsts, and also came second in the Best Kept Garden competition.

The Over Sixties Club

The Over Sixties Club was another popular club that ran for quite some time. The club was run by Mr. and Mrs Kerr. It also met in the Mission Room but when Beacon Court was built it was transferred there as most of its members were residents of the warden-controlled home.

*The Over Sixties Club preparing for a day trip outside the Mission Room
Back row, left to right: Bill Hawkins, Charlie Nightingale, Joyce Neal, Mrs Davies, Alan Davies, N/K, Dorothy Chalkley, Flo Turville, Daisy Judd, Maggie Aldridge. Front row: Gladys Howsen, May Penn, Violet George and Rene Todd.*

Sporting activities are presently well supported with the Village Hall being home to the Hertford Heath Carpet Bowls Club, and The Hertford Heath Badminton Club.

Netball Team

A Ladies Netball Team was formed in 1992 by Mrs. Maureen Perez and played informally with just a few local women in the Village School. It has since expanded, with the game being played by children and ladies alike, and has become very popular. Mrs Perez trains the seniors and Denise Jones the juniors. In 1999 it was named the Hertford Heath Rangers. The team play competitively with many members becoming extremely talented. It is affiliated to the England Netball Association.

CHAPTER THIRTEEN

Scouting in Hertford Heath

It would be correct to say that Hertford Heath had a Scout Troop from the earliest days because Haileybury College had 178 members in their troop in 1908, although they were not at that time in the Hertford District.

In 1912 a company of Boy Scouts was started by Miss Vera Barclay, the vicar's daughter, with Mr. Carter as Scoutmaster. Meetings were held the Mission Room. Hertford Heath became part of the Hertford District under the local government reorganisation of 1920, although at that time there was no Scout troop or Cub pack. The Cubs, however, restarted in 1943 when Miss Olive Valentine was enrolled as Cubmaster with 20 Cubs.

In 1942 it was also reported that a Scout Troop had been re-opened by Mr. Bishop Marshall, with 22 boys to start with and they would meet in the Church Hall.

The Scouts on 10th October 1943, in the Long Meadow. Some of those pictured here are: Peter Porley, Billy Johnson, Brian Ansell, Johnny Wren, Jimmy Turner, Lou King, Alan Kitching, Cyril Turner, Peter Claridge, Jimmy Brace, Ernie Parker, Billy Dickinson, Cyril Bell, Ian Marshall (Scoutmaster's son) and Tony Drury.

The Scouts performing Cinderella in the Village Hall in 1942 – left to right:
Wilf Mole, Johnny Wren, Alan Kitching, Lou King, Cyril Turner, Peter Claridge,
Tony Drury and Billy Dickinson.

When the local primary school was a church school, it is possible that the Headmaster, Mr. Williams, succeeded by his wife Mrs Williams, played some part in maintaining a Cub pack after the war. Esme Nix, together with Molly Walker, took over the running of the Cub pack in 1955 at a time when her son was of an age to become a Cub. Meetings were held in the Village Hall. The husbands of both Esme and Molly had been involved in Scouting, Gerald Nix being a Scoutmaster of the No 158 North London Troop at Bowes Park.

In 1969, John Walker, on the the point of retiring as Parish Clerk, was interviewed and appointed the first paid Scouting administrator by the then County Commissioner, Melville Balshillie, and the chairman, Rear Admiral John Thompson. John Walker's local influence enabled the Scout hut to be erected on land which was designated as a "children's play area". Trees were felled to clear an open space to accommodate the hut, which still stands there to this day.

County records confirm that a Cub pack was registered on 14th August 1967, with the cubmaster at that time being the primary school headmaster, Mr. B.J. Ashley. Meetings were held at the Village School where all facilities were at the disposal of the pack. Alan Burns was later to become the Cub Scout Leader (CSL). The colour of the Hertford Heath scarf at that time was navy blue and red (the Village School colours). However, in 1981 it was re-registered as an 'open' Scout group and moved to the land leased from the District Council where they set about erecting their own headquarters. A Scout troop was formed and the Cub pack became strong and active again.

A more recent stalwart has been Shirley McGinty, who was awarded a Silver Acorn in recognition of her work in maintaining an active and developing Cub group at Hertford Heath from the 70's through to the 90's. Shirley started as treasurer to the committee, and became ACSL in 1974. She resigned as CSL in 1982 and took over the administration as group secretary, she returned as Assistant Cub Scout Leader (ASCL) when Chris Searle was appointed CSL in 1987.

Alan Warman formed a Scout troop in May of 1979 with only ten Scouts. But there was a membership of 18 Scouts when a 'Foundation and Dedication Service' was held at Holy Trinity Church, Hertford Heath on 29th September 1979. This was attended by 250 people and included the local MP, Mr. Bowen Wells, County Commissioner Brigadier Freddie DeButts, District Commissioner John Bennett, and chairman of Hertford Heath Parish Council, Mr. Fred Harrington. The service was conducted by Rev. John Budd, Vicar of Hertford Heath, and Father Peter Tabernacle, Assistant Priest at St George's Church, Enfield, and Chaplain of the Guild of Servants of the Sanctuary, North London. Bill Wright succeeded as Scout Leader when Alan Warman resigned.

When the county council decided that the Scouts would have to pay rent for use of the School Hall, this persuaded them it was time to have their own headquarters. The original hut was purchased from Hertfordshire County Council for £100; it was one that had been erected alongside Gascoyne Way in Hertford, and no longer used. Shirley McGinty, CSL Robbie Hamilton and Dave Smith, the headmaster and chairman of the Scout group, along with many other willing helpers, dismantled the hut piece by piece. It was then transported and stored in a barn on land at Rush Green. The hut was not erected until 1983 due to several delays with builders for the foundations and long discussions with East Herts District Council as to a suitable site in the village. It was finally erected over many weekends, with the help of a few parents and lots of 1st Hertford Leaders and Venture Scouts who camped on the site for most of the weekends.

Changing Leaders

Robbie Hamilton and later Barbara Gibbs were CSLs to the Group whilst Shirley McGinty, Geraldine Walker and Gwen Cannon were ACSLs. Later Geraldine was persuaded to become CSL. Geraldine with the help of her husband, Ian, who took out a warrant and acted as GSL for a period, remained Akela until 1987 when she retired a little disappointed at the limited help that was forthcoming at pack meetings. Ian, in addition to taking out a warrant, also acted as chairman of the group until 1984.

Chris Searle assumed the duties of CSL when Geraldine resigned until 1989 .When he resigned as CSL he was persuaded to run the Cub Pack with Danielle Cox and Gillian Hirons.

The Hertford Heath Cubs in 1981
Top row: Mark Walker, Wayne Robinson, Duncan Newton, Christopher Parker,
Asa Newton, Benjamin Neil and Stephen Oliver.
Second row: Simon Leader, Jonathan Boulger, Jonathan Gilkes, Ian Tollett,
Sam Roberts, Paul Cannell and Gareth Henman.
Third row: Paul Capel, Graham Hirons, Dominic Macer, Gwen Cannon,
Geraldine Walker, Ben Eagling, Alister Carrington and Mark Leader.
Bottom row: Neil Oakley, Keith Phypers, Richard Cannell, Darren Shepherd,
Ian Risk, Simon Carrington and Jonathan Fisher.

Gillian and Les Hirons were initially introduced to the group through serving on the committee in the early eighties but Gillian was keen to play a more active part. She became a helper, and soon an ACSL before taking over as Akela, when she succeeded Chris Searle in 1989. Les in the meantime was elected chairman and there followed a period of about seven years when Gillian and Les played a significant part in the progress and success of the Hertford Heath Group. Les remembers a huge debt in excess of £8,000 when he became chairman, much of this resulting from the purchase of the hut and the erection and installation of services. A tremendous effort was required over the following years to raise funds and clear this debt, and enormous credit is due to all the parents and friends, plus the committee and Leaders, who not only cleared the debt but showed a significant surplus by the time Les finally gave up the chair.

With the general shortage of funds, Gillian as Akela saw the need to form an alliance with another group and this proved to be the 3rd Hertford. She remembers the generous support and co-operation received from the 3rd's and the sharing of facilities which led to the opportunity for her boys to camp at Dane Mead, Phasels, Tolmers and most significantly to attend Gilwell in 1990. Gillian enjoyed the traditional approach to Scouting with the Arrow Programme and the 'caps'. She says "the boys were as disappointed as us when the caps were no longer required as part of the uniform".

When Les Hirons resigned as chairman in 1986, the post was filled by David Bee who proved to be an inspiration to the whole group. David together with his wife, Doreen, undertook an enormous amount of hard work organising fund-raising events. His legacy was to be a very healthy bank balance. Another future ACSL was Trevor Johnson who, with Dave King and the help of parents and friends, organised events such as Christmas Fayres, Sausage Sizzles and Quiz Nights.

With Dad a 3rd Hertford Scout during the post-war period and Mum the Brown Owl at Hertford Heath, it was hardly surprising that Danielle Cox should be persuaded to help when the new hut was erected. Subsequently she became a helper to neighbour Geraldine Walker and later took out a warrant (at the same time as Gillian Hirons) before becoming Akela in 1981. Pauline Cox and Danielle Cox (married but with the same surname) have already been associated with this Group for 17 years and their continued enthusiasm is very apparent. Danielle is full of praise for the help and support from Trevor Johnson and Dave King.

Pauline's own career meant her resignation from the Guides and whilst Danielle helped with the Brownies for a while it proved not to be her forte. However, in due course the opportunity occurred for Pauline to take out a warrant and become GSL when Shirley retired in 1997. The Beavers and the Cubs are presently active in this modern age along with the Brownie Guides, and Rainbow Guides

We know there have been relatively short periods in the past when Scouts have been active on the Heath. Perhaps the new century will identify a Leader to start a Scout Section again?

CHAPTER FOURTEEN

The Hertford Heath Players

The Hertford Heath Players were formed in 1953; they put on plays concerts and Pantomimes, with the entire cast coming from Hertford Heath.

They presented their show, *Coronation Capers*, on June 13th 1953. The programme included the song "Belle of the Ball", sung by Bob Akers who was joined in the ballet dancing by Brenda Bailey. Mrs Bulley and Mrs Carrie Cox were the accompanists – Mrs Bulley was the Church organist and Mrs Cox a school teacher and accomplished pianist. A number of village children from the dance groups "The Sunbeams" and "The Rainbow Dancers", took part in the concert. The dancing was arranged by Mrs Emily Timson.

Bob Akers and Brenda Bailey in "Belle of the Ball"

Following *Coronation Capers* was the *Christmas Revue,* also put on in 1953. These concerts were held in the Gymnasium at Goldings, Hertford and halls in the surrounding areas.

Their first pantomime was *Cinderella,* which was performed in the Village Hall and surrounding villages. The players earned rave reviews from the *Hertfordshire Mercury*, who described it as a lively robust show, with plenty of slapstick humour and with the right measure of romance, dancing and singing.

The Cast of Cinderella: Joyce Akers and Edna Lewis as the Ugly Sisters, Ellen Camp as Cinderella, Valerie Windebank as the Fairy Godmother, Principal Boy Pat Langman, Bob Akers as Buttons, Bernard Budd as The Baron, Jessie Adams as Dandini. In the Chorus were Pat Turner, Fay Bamber, Pat Harrington and Valerie Barrett. The Prince's Page was Yvonne Turville.

Caroline Cox was the pianist, Eric Lewis and Cecil Aldridge looked after scenery and construction, Peggy Harvey the dancing, Gwen Pearman wardrobe and Fred Camp lighting,

Harold De Boeck was stage manager, Michael Fox sound effects and Lily Bamber costumes. The producer and writer was John C. Adams.

In February 1958 the players presented *Three One Act Plays*, consisting of 'Have You Seen My Lady?' 'The Justice of Ching San Chu' and 'Fumed Oak'. The cast was Joyce Akers, Edna Lewis, Albert Copeland, Kenneth Kitching, Rhona Cameron, Victor Chappell, Caroline Cox, Francois Jones, Bob Akers, June Sayer and Mary Denny.

In March 1959 they put on a play called *The Love Match*, for which the producer was Francois Jones, stage manager Eric Lewis and assistant stage manager Sid Pavey. The cast comprised Joyce Akers, June Sayer, Ray Evans, Victor Chappell, Albert Copeland, Stanley Blackeby, Bob Akers, Jim Beardmore and Margaret Camp. One other pantomime that the players performed was *Babes in the Woods (with Robin Hood)*. The producer was John C. Adams and the price of a programme 1d.

The cast of Babes in the Wood (with Robin Hood):
Back Row from left to right: John Foster, Edna Lewis, Brenda Bradford, Vic Chappell, Bernard Budd, Joyce Akers, Pat Langman, Gwen Pearman, Bob Akers, Anne Morris, Pauline Woodley and Yvonne Turville.
Middle Row: Fay Bamber, Janet Copps, Pat Harrington, Heather Rose, Marie Russell, Pam Cox and Jean Judd.
Front Row: Georgina Cavill, Brenda Cox, Sandra Hundleby, Evelyn Hawkins, Sheila Bird, Christine Judd and Mary Umney.

The Hertford Heath Players disbanded when television became popular and support for this type of entertainment dwindled.

MRS EMILY TIMSON

Mrs Timson is remembered fondly by many of the village people. She was a foster mother to many children. She used to live at the end of Portland Place, and taught local children how to dance. She gave up much of her time to the 'Rainbow Dancers' and 'The Sunbeams' who performed with the Hertford Heath Players. In the two groups were four of her foster children – Janet Cain, Freda Head and Anita and Julie Beirton.

Mrs Emily Timson

Mrs Timson's Sunbeams – Mary Umney, Margaret Walker, Pamela Cox, Brenda Cox, Christine Kanolty, Janet Cain, Jackie Bean, Freda Head, Marie Russell, Maureen Penn and Rosa Madden.

CHAPTER FIFTEEN

Pubs, Inns and Beerhouses

The oldest public house on the Heath is The Goat, situated on the village green. It used to be called The Goat Inn and before that would possibly have been just an alehouse. The earliest part dates from 1630 with later extensions on both sides. Troops were billeted there during the Seven Years War 1756–1763. In 1887 The Goat Inn sold Christie's Fine Ales, brewed in Hoddesdon. In 1998 Marston's were the owners and more recently Greene King.

The Goat Inn pictured in 1925, showing the Goat Cottages and the fountain on the green.

A vintage look at the men of the village sitting outside The Goat.

A ghost is reputed to haunt The Goat, moving furniture around and creating a cold atmosphere in its wake. Some of the brave tenants of the Goat have been:

Elizabeth Cordell, Mary Ann Yates, William Goddard, Charles Pigram, Mr. Charlie Callfe, Len Lewis, Tom Matthews, Mel and Mabel Bellis, John and Sheila Goold, Sue Bentley and Laz and Nada Ceko.

Pubs were mostly frequented by men, only gaining popularity with ladies after the war. Beer was from tuppence a pint, with one of the beers called Blue Jug. Brown Ale was famous in the McMullen's pubs. Games were played in the pubs, the most popular being darts, shove halfpenny, crib, skittles and dominoes. Nearly every pub had a piano, with singing along to it a must. Only one flavour of crisps was available in those days, with a little blue salt bag inside the packet – if you were lucky.

The Two Brewers

There were two other small beer houses in Downfield Road, the Horse and Dray and the Two Brewers. In 1895 Henry Akers was the beer retailer at the Horse and Dray and in 1901 Frederick Pamphlion. When the pub closed it was converted into a residential dwelling occupied by Mrs Hawkins, who also did hairdressing from the house. The Two Brewers was originally called The Brewers Arms in 1868. It closed in 1962 when the property was sold by Noah Young of Hertford.

At the time this picture was taken Downfield Road was called Ware Road, and later The Street. The Two Brewers is to the left of the picture postcard, which shows the Benskins sign with Mrs. Farnham standing in front of the pub. Hillcrest Terrace is centre right in the picture, with Rose Porter and husband Fred standing at the gate of number three.

Some of the tenants of The Two Brewers have been Mrs Susan Brown, James Childs, George F. Cox, Jack Mole and Fred and Mick Lingwood.

The Havelock Arms

The Havelock Arms, in London Road, was built in 1817 by Peter Cleophas, a butler from Haileybury College, who was part West Indian. It was named after Major-Gen. Sir Henry Havelock, K.C.B., who distinguished himself in the Indian Mutiny from 1795-1857. The first picture shows Mr. Frank Turner who along with his wife Edith were the tenants during the 1950's. His son, Ron (Digger) Turner, was in the Fire Service during the war and some of the Turner family still reside on the Heath. The pub closed in 1963. Some of the other tenants have been Bert Pearce, George Locking and Mr. Brown

An old postcard showing the Havelock Arms and London Road.

The Townshend Arms

The Townshend Arms was built in 1823 right across the line of the Roman road of Ermine Street. It replaced The Green Man which was on a site about 200 yards away, owned by the Dunster family of Jenningsbury; on the death of Henry Dunster in 1792, it was sold to Richard Flower, the Hertford brewer. The licence was transferred to the newly built public house, the Townshend Arms in 1823, and it adopted the arms of the Viscount Townshend, owner of Balls Park. The old building was later demolished and its site acquired by the vicarage. The war memorial dominates the scenery in front of the building.

Little has changed from this old postcard to the present day.

Some of the tenants of the Townshend Arms have been: Thomas Ballard, James Childs, Rebecca Childs, John Smith, Jack Smith, Mr. Leigh, Renee Gibbs, John and Joyce Marshgreen, Fred Lingwood and Bunny and Doreen Bunyan.

One incident that took place in and outside the Townshend Arms on 22nd September 1855 was recorded in the Hertfordshire Gleanings. The dramatic headline in the *Hertfordshire Mercury* was "MANSLAUGHTER AT HERTFORD HEATH". The story unfolded as the trial examined evidence and the newspaper carried the following report.

George Kiff, aged 25, labourer, Little Amwell, was charged with the Manslaughter of Thomas Godfrey, at Hertford Heath. Mr. Bushby conducted the case for the prosecution; Mr. O'Brien defended the prisoner.

John Brown exclaimed: "I was at the Townshend Arms Public House, at Hertford Heath, on 22nd September last."

Mr. Justice Crompton: "What night was it?"

Witness: "Saturday night."

Mr. Justice Crompton: "Thought so. Nearly all these cases of manslaughter occur at the public house on Saturday night, when men who have just received their money go and spend it on drink, instead of taking it home."

Examination continued: "There were several persons in the house at the time. The prisoner and Godfrey were there; they both worked for Mr. Trustram. A man named Smith, who also worked for Mr. Trustam was there and, in the course of conversation, remarked that he and Godfrey were Mr. Trustram's best men. Kiff did not say anything at the time, and soon left the house. He shortly afterwards returned, and had not been in the house long before he pulled off his coat and said 'I'll let you know who is the best man'. He then hit Smith with his open hand, and turned to Godfrey and gave him a blow. I got hold of the prisoner, and he rushed out of my hands and flew at Godfrey again. Then they got to fighting, and both fell down, Godfrey being underneath. I got hold of the prisoner and the landlord of the Townshend Arms took up Godfrey. The landlord said he would have no disturbance in his house, and I then let Kiff go. Godfrey had in the meantime left the house, and Kiff went out saying 'where is he?' He then rushed at Godfrey and knocked him down. I went and got hold of Kiff and held him. Godfrey did not show any signs of life after this; I did not see him move afterwards, nor hear him speak. Both Kiff and Godfrey were somewhat tipsy, but Kiff was the worst."

Cross examined by Mr. O'Brien: "When Kiff went towards Godfrey the second time, Godfrey did not get up to meet him. Godfrey was standing by the side of the table with his fists clenched. Godfrey had been out of the house about five minutes before Kiff went out. When Kiff got out the door Godfrey was standing about two or three yards from the water-trough. Kiff went directly up to him with his fist on the left side of the neck. I did not see Kiff kick him; I don't think Kiff had anything in his hand when he struck Godfrey. It was a moonlight night."

George Smith examined: "I was at the Townshend Arms on Saturday night the 22nd of September. When I said that I and Godfrey were Mr. Trustram's best men, Kiff came to me and hit me in the face; he then went to Godfrey and struck him. Godfrey and Kiff had a struggle in the room; the landlord said he would have no row in the house. Godfrey went out and Stalley with him. I went out afterwards and saw Kiff hit Godfrey once. Godfrey fell down and never got up again."

Mr. P. Reilly, surgeon, of Hertford, examined: "About one o'clock in the morning, the 23rd September, I was called in to see the deceased; he was quite dead and cold. I examined the head and found a slight abrasion of the skin of the cheek. I afterwards made a *post mortem* examination. I was assisted by Mr. Davies and my brother. On moving the scalp on the left hand side above the ear, we found a fracture of the skull, where there was a quantity of congealed blood. We removed the skull and examined the back portion of the brain. We found the *medulla oblongata* separated from the *cerebellum*, which was sufficient in itself to cause instant death. The brain was in a very congested state. The injury might have been occasioned by a fall or a blow."

Mr. O'Brien addressed the jury for the prisoner and called Mr, Trustram, farmer, who stated that the prisoner had worked for him for some years and he has always considered him a peaceable, well disposed man.

Mr. Justice Crompton, in summing up, remarked that the only question for the jury was whether Godfrey's fall, which appeared to have caused his death, was the result of any unlawful violence on the part of Kiff? It was no justification for Kiff that Godfrey had showed a disposition to fight, for the fight itself was an unlawful act. It must not be supposed that if two men get drunk and quarrel and fight, and the death of one of them is the result, the other is not guilty of manslaughter, merely because they were engaged in what is called a fair fight. It was not lawful for two men, even though they both agreed to fight, to use violence towards each other. Whether, therefore, the deceased fell in consequence of a blow or a push from Kiff, it did not affect the question of his guilt. According to the evidence, it would appear that the deceased did not fall the last time in consequence of a blow; but the simple question was whether he fell from any act of violence of any kind on the part of the prisoner?

The jury returned the following verdict: Guilty of manslaughter in its mildest form. Mr. Justice Crompton, in passing sentence, said this certainly was not an aggravated case of manslaughter, for it appeared to him that Godfrey wanted to fight as well as the prisoner, and in the fight the prisoner exhibited no brutality such as kicking his antagonist. The prisoner was very sorry that he had been the cause of the death of his companion. As the prisoner had been in prison nearly three months, the sentence would be a comparatively light one. Sentence was to be imprisonment for one month.

The George Kiff referred to was the son of John Kiff and Martha Goldsmith, christened on 11th April 1830 at All Saints Church Hertford.

The College Arms

From about 1780 until 1808 there was a pub called The Jolly Pindar on the site of The College Arms. It was just a small alehouse and was said to be on the highest point between London and York. The name was taken from the nearby pound, where the Pindar of the village would impound animals that were grazing on the Heath without proper authority. When the East India Company decided to build their college on the Heath, the alehouse was rebuilt to twice its size and called the Old East India College Arms (Hotel). In 1999 the current owners decided to change its name back to The Jolly Pindar.

THE OLD EAST INDIA COLLEGE ARMS HOTEL. HERTFORD HEATH   HTD. 54

Some of the tenants of the College Arms have been: Frederick Bowman Moore, William Hillier, William Mansfield, James Tebby, Thomas Tulley, John Coulson, James Henry Moore, Mr. Mortimer, Mr. Comer, David Cameron, Mrs E Wakeling, John and Betty Buckley and Severio Caroleo from 1990 to 2007.

The Jolly Pindar was transformed in the year 2007 and reopened once again as The College Arms.

The Crown Public House

The Crown Public House in London Road was built in about 1839. It was owned by William Manser and occupied by John Henry Rann. It was subsequently sold to McMullen's of Hertford, who were the owners until 1991. It had a smithy to one side and Arthur Fletcher worked there and ran the pub at the same time in 1895. There was also a wooden building on the car park used as a shop. Mr. Rogers used it as a cobbler's shop and later Mr. Frank Turner for selling fruit and vegetables. When McMullen's sold the pub, the new owners renamed it The Silver Fox.

Here is a photograph of a coach outing with locals posing in front of the Crown taken in about 1950.

Back row, left to right: Maze Dawes, Wally Cast, Wally's Mum, Una Cast, Rose Camp, Charlie Camp, Dora Miles, Rose Hornett, May Porter, Margaret Brown, ? , ? , Pat Porter, Maisie Shepherd, Fred Porter, Anna Shepherd, Les Shepherd, Bert Pomphret, Lou King, Jim Locking, Auriole Boreham/Wilcher, George Wilcher, Den Wilcher and the driver.
Front row: Wally Childs, Stan Smith, Jack Turville, Fred Brown, Alice Penn, Lil Wilcher, Mrs Phypers, Tiddler Turner, Joan Turner, Albert Turville, Bill Brown and Vince Thompson.

The Crown in 1980

Some of the tenants of The Crown have been: Arthur Fletcher, Andrew Cotton, Sarah Webb, Henry Wareham, Henry (Harry) Boreham, George and Bubbles Martin and Horace Hales.

The Crown in 1912 with the Blacksmith's in the background and what was to become the Post Office in the foreground.

The Galley Hall

Although not actually within Hertford Heath, the Galley Hall has a great deal of history that is connected to the Heath and was and is still well known by the locals. 'Galley' is a dialect form of the word gallows. It began as a farmhouse called Collewelle Haugh (or Haw meaning an enclosure) in 1374, and by 1765 was known as the Galley Hall. One of its farmers was Edward Hunsdon, responsible for the Hailey Bushes land and sheep.

It became an inn about 1830 and was run by Benjamin Logsdale. A deed conveyed it to Christie Cathrow, brewers of Hoddesdon, in 1837. The tenants of the Galley Hall also managed a grub shop which was at the far end of the pub where there is now the kitchen. Food was served through a window with hot potatoes and saveloys being much appreciated by the college boys. Also many years ago there used to be a garage where the car park is now situated.

The Galley Hall in 1902, with Frank and Susan Watson as proprietors.

The Galley Hall pictured in 2006

Some of the tenants of the Galley Hall have been, Frank Watson, Susan Watson, Mrs Julia Hobbs, Mr. Hay and Terry Scales.

CHAPTER SIXTEEN

Characters of the Village

There have been many people who will be remembered for years to come for either their achievements or just being someone that had that unique something which made them memorable. We have had many councillors that have worked loyally for the village, among them Fred Harrington, Lillian Bean, Lesley Wren and Gerald Nix.

Fred Harrington served on the Parish Council for over 40 years, 30 of them as Clerk. He was also for 22 years the village's representative on the Hertford Rural District Council where he served on a number of committees including planning and housing. He was at one time chairman of the rural council and secretary of the Labour Party, working alongside Bob Sibley who was chairman. He was married to Millie and they had three children, Fred Jnr, Pat and Wendy. The block of 20 flats built in Trinity Road was named Harrington Court in honour of Fred.

Fred Harrington with his wife Millie and daughter Wendy at a Buckingham Palace Garden Party in 1962 when he was chairman of the Hertford Rural District Council and, on the right, pictured after his retirement.

Lily Bean served on served on several committees of local organisations including the Women's Institute, the Horticultural Society, the Labour Party, and the Royal British Legion. She was a Parish Councillor and a stalwart of the church. Lily's husband Stan was also on the Parish Council and the Horticultural Society and was a member of the Cricket Club.

Mr. and Mrs Wren with Mr. and Mrs Bean

Leslie Wren served on the Parish Council during his time on the village and supported the Horticultural Society. His business as the local baker in Downfield Road made him a respected and prominent member of the local community.

Gerald Nix was a Parish Councillor, served as chairman for several years and was the local District Councillor from 1983-1991. He was also a member of the Village Hall Committee. His wife, Esme, was a teacher at Herford Heath School and a member of the W.R.V.S., helping with the delivery of Meals on Wheels. She was very interested in the village history and wrote an informal booklet called *Washerwomen to Launderette,* some of which was included in the book, *Pond Dipping*, produced by the Women's Institute of which she was a member.

Olive Davison, who lived in Trinity Road, was well known for serving on many committees among them the Village Fête and the Horticultural Society. In earlier years, she was an active member of the Girl Guides and was the secretary of the Royal British Legion for many years. Olive's husband, Henry, also served on the Horticultural Society and was chairman for a number of years. He was a bus driver for over thirty years and served as chairman of the Transport and General Workers Union at Hertford bus garage.

Ernest and Jean Kerr, who lived in Mount Pleasant, were well known for their dedication to the village and served in many ways. Ernest was a Parish Councillor and treasurer of the Horticultural Society for some years. They helped to start the Over-60 club in the late 1950's and put in a lot of effort in helping to run the club for many years after its formation. Jean was a member of the church congregation where she served in many capacities.

Nurse Ethel Dean was our local and much loved District Nurse, who often cycled to visit her patients in the village. She lived in a cottage along London Road, opposite the Priors Wood Road junction. All the children she brought into the world were special to her and she seemed to remember them even when they had grown up. Nurse Dean lived to a good age, remaining active after her retirement, including walking to church every Sunday.

Nurse Dennison was another well known midwife, who lived in St. Margaret's and will be remembered by many mothers from the Heath for her kindness and dedication to them in childbirth and continued support in the months after.

Many will remember **Mrs Doris Bulley** who lived in the one of the cottages in the Vicarage Causeway. She was the church organist for 52 years and an active member of the Over-60 club. She also played the piano accordion.

One of the old characters of the village was **Charles Rand,** who lived in London Road and whose nickname was 'Randy'. One of his favourite hobbies was attending jumble sales in the village and elsewhere collecting clothing, household goods, tools and many other items. These were stored in every room of the house and if there was any item that you wanted, he would almost always be able to find it for you. He had hundreds of items in the house but he always seemed to know where to look for what you required. Mr. Rand had an old bicycle with a large trailer attached to the back and this would be piled high with his purchases from the jumble sales. He was sometimes joined by a lady, called Kate Cast, who also had a bicycle and they would attend the sales together. She had a wicker basket on the front of her bike which she would fill with jumble. Mr. Rand had a few run-ins with the local constables, mainly for riding his bicycle on the pavement. On one occasion he came out of Hertford Heath Stores and rode his bike along the pavement, hotly pursued by PC MacLean who lived in the police house near the shop. Mr. Rand eventually stopped opposite the College Arms where PC MacLean told him he was breaking the law. Mr. Rand laughed heartily and told the constable he ought to have better things to do. He was, not for the first time let off with a caution. He lived into his nineties and died about 1965.

Bill Brown (Bunty) lived all of his life in London Road and will be remembered for his good humour and wit. He was born in 1925 and was jailed in the war at the age of 18, for refusing to work in the mines as a Bevin Boy. He wanted to do his bit for the war effort, but refused to go into the coal mines and was jailed not once but twice in Bedford Prison. Realising he would never capitulate after his second stint behind bars, the authorities allowed him to join the army as a private in the Beds and Herts Regiment serving in India. On demob he worked at Taylor Walker's Hoddesdon brewery depot as a drayman.

Bill was a true country man and with his dog, Sandy, was proud to be the bane of gamekeepers. He boasted that he had never been caught poaching because his dog could detect a policeman or gamekeeper at 200 yards, day or night. He kept and used ferrets to catch rabbits, and was a good shot with his rifle. After his retirement he worked as a keeper for a small private pheasant shooting syndicate, overseeing the welfare of the birds. He would patrol the pens with his dog at first light to check for possible damage by foxes or other dangers. He enjoyed pub games, like dominoes and cards, and was well known in village hostelries; one of his favourite pubs was The Huntsman at Goose Green in Hoddesdon. He died age 76, but will be always be remembered by his friends and family.

Bill Brown in India   *Bill and Lou King*   *Den Wilcher*

One of Bill's closest friends was **Lou King,** who lived a short distance from him and shared his love of country life. Lou was a colourful character with a wide repertoire of songs that he would sing, especially on coach outings (some more daring than others) but they made all the passengers laugh. Lou also worked for Taylor Walker's and later the Milk Marketing Board. Lou would go out in all weathers with Bill and Bob Kimpton to catch rabbits. He was a keen greyhound enthusiast and kept a retired greyhound called Magic Dust. Greyhounds and whippets used to be raced on Sundays in Hertford Heath on the Sports Field. To train them a bicycle was rigged up on a stand with a winder in place of the back wheel, attached to a long cord trailing a rabbit skin. After the dogs had gone down to the bottom of the field someone would sit on the bike and peddle pulling the rabbit skin for the dogs to chase. They were then considered ready to be raced at Rye House Stadium.

Den Wilcher will be remembered for his ability to play the spoons which he did in all the pubs on the village. He was born in the old public house in Downfield Road called the Horse and Dray.

Clarice Nellie Pawsey lived at Amwell Place Farm and was our local poet. She died in 1979, aged 82, but her poems live on and are treasured by her daughter, Jean Hundleby. She penned many a famous poem one of which she put to music and won the British finals of the Country Women of the World theme song competition. The Country Women of the World was an association to which the British Women's Institution was affiliated.

Mr. and Mrs Pawsey on their 50th wedding anniversary.

The Countrywoman's Song

We do not want to rule the world
Or force our views on others
We only seek to speed the day
When men will live as brothers.

Though widely scattered as we are
Each in her native land,
Our common problems cares and doubts
We'll try to understand.

For understanding, we believe
Will bring about release
From constant fear of war's alarm
And help the world to peace.

Clarice Nellie Rebentisch, one of four children, was born in Southend in 1897; her father was of German ancestry and her mother English. The family moved to Edmonton and then on to Broxbourne. She was a teacher for three years at St.Paul's School, Hoddesdon. She met her husband-to-be Arthur Pawsey at a dance in Rye House. He had been wounded during the First World War and had been invalided out to the old Hertford Barracks. What drew them together was the fact that he was born a Suffolk man, born just outside Bury St. Edmund's, and her mother was a Suffolk woman, so they got on well together.

They married on June 14, 1923 at St.Augustine's Church Broxbourne and went straight to live at Amwell Place Farm, Hertford Heath where they stayed for forty years. During that time they did not have one night away from the farm. In 1973 they celebrated their fiftieth wedding anniversary.

They had one daughter Jean who lives in the house that her parents lived in after they left the farm. The house in Downfield Road is reputed to be the oldest house on the village, it was built in 1610 and was nicknamed Cosy Cott by Mrs. Pawsey.

Mrs. Pawsey was a woman of many talents, as well as her poetry she taught

127

the piano and wrote music and wrote her memoirs in her infamous own style. She wrote both the words and music of a wedding hymn for her granddaughter's wedding. She took an active interest in village life. She was a member of the W.I., the Mother's Union and the Hertford Music Club. She was also the secretary of the Over 60's Club. For many years she was the *Hertfordshire Mercury's* correspondent for Hertford Heath. At the age of 72 Mrs. Pawsey took a course in authorship "Writing for pleasure and profit" at Denham College.

Two of Mrs. Pawsey's poems

Beatitudes for the Elderly

Blessed are they who understand
My faltering steps and shaking hand.
Blessed, who know my ears to-day
Must strain to catch the things they say
Blessed are they who seem to know
My eyes are dim, and my mind is slow.
Blessed are they, who look away
When tea is spilled on the cloth that day.
Blessed are they with a cheery smile
Who stopped to chat for a little while.
Blessed are they who never say
"You've told that story twice to-day".
Blessed are they who make it known
That I'm loved, respected, and not alone.
And blessed are they who ease the days
Of my journey home, in loving ways.

To Bring Contentment

A Visit for an hour or so
Is not much to give,
yet what a difference it makes
to cheer them while they live.

A flower, a gift, a birthday card
a kindly word of praise,
Will bring contentment
and brighten up their days.

Don't push the aged on one side
Nor leave them in the cold
Remember, if you're spared as well
You, too, will grow old.

So while you have it in your power
And while they're with you still
Make life as easy as you can,
And Christian love fulfil.

CHAPTER SEVENTEEN

The Pindar of the Manor

For generations there had been a Pindar or Hayward of the Manor. The appointment was made by the Lord or Lady of the Manor. Since 1901, when Haileybury College became Lord of the Manor, the Bursar of the College made the appointment. The post was considered to be an important one, and his duties were to take the usual fees for the grazing of livestock on the Heath from farmers and small holders excising their Commoners' rights and to impound those animals that were on the Heath without proper authority. The Roundings could be completely enclosed by the three sets of gates that were in place there, one just past the College Arms at the entrance to the Roundings, one at the far side near Rose Cottage, Elbow Lane, and one behind the garage in London Road. His other duties were to protect the turf, minerals, gravel, underwood and timber as only certain people had the right to cut faggots and take brushwood.

On 18th July 1895, William Hayden was approved to be Pindar of the Manor by Alice Charrington. She was Lady of the Manor of Great Amwell and the wife of Spencer Calmeyers Charrington Esq., of Winchfield Lodge, Winchfield in the County of Southampton. His pay was two pounds per annum payable on the eleventh day of May. When he retired he was succeeded by his grandson, John (Jack) Hayden.

In 1916 Jack Hayden became involved in a dispute with Mr. E. Anson, the Bursar of Haileybury College, who had erected a notice board at the entrance to the Roundings with the words "Private Road" printed on it. This sparked off an argument with the villagers as to whether this would infringe their rights to graze cattle there. Mr. Anson explained that the notice was to discourage large motor lorries from using the road, as the College had to maintain it. Legal advice was sought and H.W. Lathom, solicitors, gave assurance that the rights of the Commoners could not be taken away, and their grazing rights would remain. This case was successful for the villagers.

A public inquiry was held some years later, when once more the Governors of the College wished to impose "limitations on and conditions as to the waste of the Manor of Great Amwell (Hertford Heath)." This is the report published in the *Hertfordshire Mercury*:

A Ministry of Agriculture and Fisheries public inquiry was held at Haileybury College, Hertford Heath, on Wednesday with regard to a proposal of the Governors of the College as Lords of the Manor of Great Amwell, to impose "limitations on and conditions as to the exercise of rights of public access to the waste of the Manor of Great Amwell (Hertford Heath)". The limitations asked for by the college included the prohibition of the removal of wood, turf, etc. from the Common, the grazing of horses, cattle, etc. (not belonging to a Commoner) on the land: the breaking in of horses; deposit of litter; bathing in any stream, shooting etc.

The Inspector conducting the inquiry was Mr. Cyril Wood Hill, assistant legal advisor to the Ministry; Mr. Bowyer, counsel, appeared for the Governors, with Mr. Philip Longmore; Messrs A. Odell and E.A. Bailey, members of the Great Amwell Parish Council, represented their council; Mr. E.W. Bowers of the Little Amwell Parish Council represented a number of villagers and Mr. John Longmore, clerk of Hertford Rural Council, attended of behalf of his council.

Mr. Bowyer said the subject of the enquiry was the waste land of the Manor of Great Amwell, extending for some 68 acres – consisting of the Roundings (about 25 acres) and Hertford Heath. In March of last year, the Governors executed a deed under the Law of Property Act and later the Governors made an application to the Minister for an order to be made regulating the right of the public use of the land and imposing certain limitations. Five local authorities were affected by the Order, the Herts County Council, the Rural Councils of Hertford and Ware, and the Parish Councils of Great and Little Amwell. All had approved the proposed order with the exception of Great Amwell.

COMMONERS' RIGHTS

The rights of Commoners, said Mr. Bowyer, would not be interfered with. The Order was subject to any rights the Commoners might have, such as grazing cattle, etc.

Addressing the Inspector, Mr. Bowers for Little Amwell Parish Council said that when the notice containing the limitations was posted, a petition signed by 152 Hertford Heath residents was sent to the Ministry opposing limitations. There were people, he said, of 90 and 75 years of age who had been doing things it was proposed to limit for years, although they had no common rights.

The Inspector intimated that the question of common rights could not enter the scope of the inquiry, but Mr. Bowers replied that it would do a great deal to clear the question up. Speaking as an ordinary member of the public he said he thought the limitations were harsh. It was proposed to fine people 40s if dogs were chasing game, and the same amount for bird nesting. Children were prevented from bathing in the streams which they had done for years.

Replying to a question, the Bursar of the College, Major B.M.S. Foljambe, said there were only nine Commoners. Mr. Odell said he thought that the power to impose limitations should be in the hands of a public authority and not a private body. The Great Amwell Parish Council were not very pleased with the College in general and were rather sceptical whether the limitations would stop as proposed.

Inspector: "Well, they won't be able to go any further unless they get a further order. Mr. Odell said it was stated that no cart could go on the Common, If this were so how could access be obtained to the farm and cottages on the Common? According to a map there were 80 acres of this land. what had happened to the other 12 acres? Mr. Bowyer said that the order would take away rights people have had for 60 years. Inspector: Are you frightened that in administering this Order the Governors of the College will act in an improper way? Mr. Odell: I should not like to go so far as to say in an improper way, but if they want anything they would say 'thank you very much'.

Later Mr. Odell observed that the whole of the limitations were trivial. The Inspector pointed out that under the deed the College had executed, members of the public had right of access for air and exercise, subject to complying with the law as to lighting fires, etc. If the Order, applied by the College was approved, the public would have to observe those conditions as well. Whatever happened they could not alter the first part, which was made under an Act of Parliament. Mr. Bailey said that the Order would take away the rights people had had for 60 years. Mr. Philip Longmore said that in 1916 he was deputy steward of the Manor and held an inquiry to ascertain how many Commoners there were and he allowed nine claims. Major Foljambe said that people became Commoners by ownership of property. The Inspector suggested that those people who claimed Commoner's rights should get in touch with Mr. Longmore on the subject.

But is it was all in vain. On behalf of the Hertford Rural Council Mr. John Longmore supported the Order, and said that this particular section of the Act had been applied in other places with success. The Inspector then closed the enquiry.

Jack Hayden, pictured on the left, retired as Pindar in 1935 and became a swimming pool attendant at Haileybury College. On the 4th April 1935, Mr. John (Jack) E. Hipgrave, on the right with his dog, Trimmer, was appointed Jack Hayden's successor as Pindar. He was the last man to hold this post and retired in 1948. He then took over full time farming of Pondside Farm, in Mount Pleasant.

These ancient grazing rights have since lapsed and the Roundings has reverted to natural woodland, which has now evolved into a Nature Reserve. However the lordship of the manor is still important in making the Governors of Haileybury College the rightful guardians of the Heath.

The list of Commoners' rights dated 23rd March 1916

MANOR OF GREAT AMWELL.

List of COMMON RIGHTS allowed at Manor Court held 23rd March 1916.

Name of Person.	Address.	Whether right Person or annexed to property	Limits of such Right.
Sarah Huson.	Back Row Hertford Heath.	Annexed to Meadow called "Guys Close" on borders of the Heath?	12 Horned Cattle and 1 Horse, 1 load of brush-wood a year. Pigs and Poultry.
Edgar George	New Zealand Cottages Hertford Heath.	Personal. *Deceased.*	16 Horned Cattle 4 Horses Pigs and Poultry
John Hayden	Portland Place Hertford Heath.		10 Horned Cattle 2 Horses and Pigs.
Frank Robert Potkins	Pondside Hertford Heath.	Personal	3 Horned Cattle and 2 Horses.
C Childs.	Hertford Heath.	do	10 Horned Cattle and 2 Horses.
- Wright	The Roundings Hertford Heath.	do *Deceased*	1 Horse.
Henry Brace	The Street Hertford Heath?	do	4 Horses.
Charles Dawes.	Hertford Heath.	do	1 Donkey
Trustram King.	Hertford Heath.	do *Deceased*	5 Horses and Poultry.
George Ramsey.	Hertford Heath.	do	1 Goat (tied up)

Williams Hayden's agreement as Pindar of the Manor from Mrs. Alice Charrington, Lady of the Manor of Great Amwell 1895.

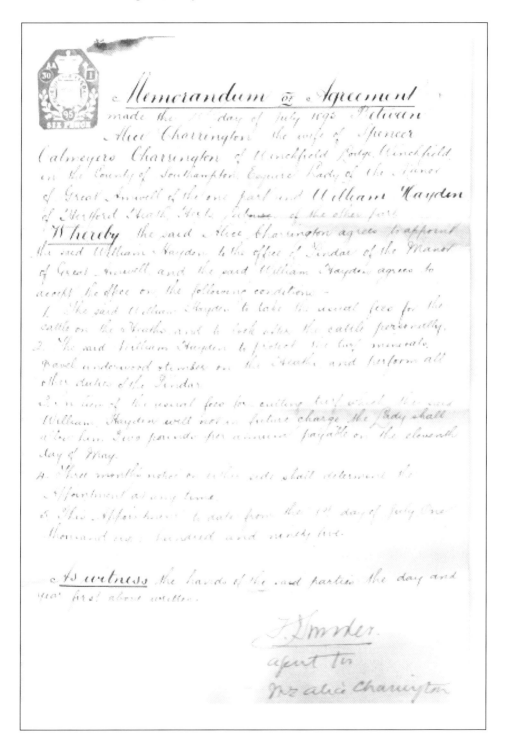

CHAPTER EIGHTEEN

Two World Wars

First World War 1914-1918

There are very few people in the village who have first-hand memories of the First World War, but a few still remember some of their relative's war-time experiences.

During the war there were services of intercession held each morning at a quarter past nine in the village church. The Rev. Charles Barclay would read out the chief war news, which was followed by appropriate prayers. The music at this little service was chosen by Florence Barclay. It consisted of a carefully chosen hymn, "Abide with me" being sung very softly, or even the song "Tipperary" which had become almost sacred to many anxious hearts.

Letter written in the Parish Magazine January 1915 by Charles W. Barclay:

THE WAR

We have to record one bright young life given in the service of his King. **Harry West** has fallen in action, killed instantaneously by a bullet through the head, a merciful painless death. He had been sent out comparatively soon after enlistment, and had not been long at the front. One of his Hertford Heath friends, writing from the front to me a few days ago, says with respect to him, "I feel it on account of knowing him so well, but I suppose we shall be fortunate if he is the only one from the Heath that gets killed in action – anyway its better than stopping at home." If that is the spirit in which our Hertford Heath men have gone to the front, we may indeed feel proud of them. It may be that some young men, who are hesitating whether or no they shall listen to the King's urgent call for men, will think over these brave words with respect to a noble death on the battlefield: *"anyway it's better than stopping at home."*

How can any young man, who is free to go, possibly stay home? So many do not realise how great and terrible this war actually is. It is no light matter, but a fight for civilisation, for all the principles of right and justice, for our homes and for our families, for the honour and the glory of England, and I verily believe for our God. England is not fighting for gain. She has entered on this war from the purest of motives possible; she is giving of her best life blood lavishly. From every class of society, men are flocking to give their services and their lives if need be for the great cause. Never before has such a war taken place in then world, and never a war of such magnitude or with such momentous results. We can thank God that so large a number of our young men have gone willingly, eagerly to do their part. Some have returned wounded, **James Akers**, who has made a good recovery [though he died later] and will soon be at the Front again: also **James Jordon** shot clean through the lungs, but is making a recovery fast, now in his home, but expecting to go again and do further service for his King.

The latest recruit is **Walter Strange,** our Church Clerk and caretaker. No doubt we shall greatly miss him while he is away, but there has been no lack of willing helpers to take up different parts of his duties in Church and School. He makes the eightieth man from Hertford Heath; if the whole of England had offered in the same proportion, it would have meant no less than three and half millions of men in our forces.

The Vicarage suffered some damage during the war by the London-bound Zeppelins that used to pass straight over Hertford Heath and return that way, too; and so did the Gotha's.

It was at 1am on September 3rd 1916 when the Zeppelin was returning that it landed and rocked the ground, causing broken glass and plaster in the Vicarage, the lawn in front of the house was covered with debris-stones, earth and bits of bomb. A crater, 12 feet across, yawned in the little meadow; on its edge the shattered body of a mare, her foal standing in the crater badly injured; blood everywhere, and the foal smell of lyddite fumes filling the air. But thankfully no human lives were lost.

At intervals of about 25 yards there were four smaller craters. These were all among the houses, but not one bomb had hit a house: they had fallen in a field, a lane, and a garden and done no harm, beyond scattering a good many tiles and killing some ducks.

Locals standing in the crater left by the Zeppelin
in Sacrament Lane (now Portland Place)

The War Memorial

The last act of generosity that Florence Barclay performed before she left the village, with her husband, was to instigate and help finance the erection of the stone cross in memory of the fallen heroes of Hertford Heath

The War Memorial was built in November 1920 with money from a fund set up for the cross, with more money being donated from the churchyard fund, and Mrs Florence Barclay making up the balance. The cross was an exact copy of the cross of St. Martin at Iona. The words etched on the cross are "Greater love hath no man than this that a man lay down his life for his friends". The whole village, a thousand people turned out for the service. A military band, and the ex-service men marching in fours, gave a martial note to the proceedings.

Two hundred men were sent to war from Hertford Heath and 34 never returned, with three more dying from their wounds after their return. The men that gave their lives were:

Arthur Akers, Charles Akers, James Akers, Henry Akers, William G. Brown, William Camp, Joshua R. Camp, Frank Chapman, Cecil Chandler, Frank Childs, Charles H. Coles, Frederick J. Coles, George Coles, Sidney J. Cox, Arthur A. Fletcher, Thomas S. Fletcher, William Gee, Chas J. Gray, Horace Gray, John W. Huson, William H. Huson, George W. Ives, Harry E. Judd, John Judd, Thomas Locking, William Middleton, Abel Pomfret, Harold E.F. Turner, Fredk. G.. Ward, Henry West and William H. West.

The three men who died from their wounds were: William E.Bulley, Charles Pratt and Albert Croft.

Every year on the Sunday nearest Armistice Day, the 11th November, a brief service is held at the War Memorial to remember those from the village who died in action in the two world wars.

Mr. and Mrs. Pyle, who lived in The Street (Downfield Road) during the First World War with their daughters. The younger one, Lucy Pyle, here aged 2, was well known for being a post woman, and later serving in the Post Office Stores (now known as the top shop) in London Road for many years.

Second World War 1939-1945

Here are the experiences of some Hertford Heath men and women during the Second World War.

Ron and Elsie Childs

Ron Childs ws born in 1919 in Hailey Lane; he was one of five children. During his childhood the family lived in the cottages in Priors Wood Road, which were situated across the top of the road that is now Postwood Green. Later when he married his wife, Elsie, he moved to Woodland Road where they had one son, Derek. He moved to his present home in London Road twenty two years ago.

Ron served in the Royal Artillery as a staff sergeant during the war and was sent to North Africa, Iraq, India, the Western Desert, Italy Monte Cassino and was home for the D-Day landing. He was wounded three times, once in each campaign and was received many decorations, among them the Military Medal. His most treasured possession is the 21st Army Group Certificate presented to him by Field Marshal Montgomery on the 23rd of May 1944.

When war was declared in September 1939, Elsie Childs, who had a typing speed of 115 words per minute, was one of a dozen shorthand-typists that were selected to work in an underground typing pool at Admiralty Arch, Whitehall. Her arrival coincided with Winston Churchill's appointment to the War Cabinet as First Lord of the Admiralty. The group lived underground for a month at a time, with only short breaks above ground, and they were sworn to secrecy. With an office opposite Mr. Churchill's, Mrs Childs saw him at close quarters after he became Prime Minister in May 1940, and masterminded the war effort. She recalled how "he wanted things done there and then and on the dot".

Ron's war experiences are recalled here in his own words. In 1939, I joined the 86th Herts Yeomany Battery. I was sent to the East Coast and posted to coastal service at Yoxford, Westleton, Saxmunden and Orford, patrolling up and down the beach day and night for protection from a possible invasion.

I was sent to the big city, London. I arrived at Scotch Barracks, Albany Street, and the next morning I was sent to the Polytechnic in Regent Street, where I remained for training in gun fitting and motor transport, as I was a motor mechanic by trade. I did not mind this as it was like going back to school. I passed out there with no trouble and was sent back to my unit, which had then moved to Morpeth, Northumberland.

I had only been back a week or so, and was then sent back to London – Woolwich, where I was sent to school again in the Military College of Science. I was there for three weeks during which time war was declared. I was then sent on to Hanley, Stoke-on-Trent to be trained on all Royal Artillery weapons; another three to four weeks there marching from one class to another. Then came the best bit: "you have passed" you can go back to your unit. "Good". I arrived there to be told not to unpack but report to the battery office. When I entered the battery office, the sergeant I saw handed me an envelope and said on your way again, this time to Nottingham. Well I never went back as I was drafted to the Middle East.

There I joined the 121 Regiment, 275 Battery. My knees were white, I did not blend in at all, as these boys had been out there some time in Iraq. I got used to it in a few days. We were sent to Baghdad, the Kurdish mountains, Mosul, Kirkuk, into Persia and then on to Egypt. The Germans under Field Marshal Rommel had launched an attack on the Suez Canal and General Ritchie's counter attack had failed, so now we had to take action up and down the desert. We went into Tobruk under two or three Generals, the last one being Montgomery. From the Nile and El Alamein to Tunis. we were in action until we reached Enfidaville where it was all hell let loose. After El Alamein we were called AGRA for short (Army Group of Royal Artillery). Where there was trouble we went into action about six regiments altogether. At one time I was in the Long Range Desert Group. We in the Eighth Army always finished the job.

We went on to Sidi Bou Ali and then on to a victory parade in Tunis, and then back to Tripoli and Eldjem. Most of this was with 10 Corps under the command of General B.G. Horrocks. We took part in the invasion of Italy with 5 AGRA. We went in to Sicily (not a bad landing) and then into Palermo.

After we got consolidated, there we went back out in our landing ship and tanks to Tripoli and with us went the Yanks – they did not like our rations of biscuits and bully beef. We sailed through the Straits of Messina at Salerno; the Sicilian Cliffs were hard to climb. I think this was one of the worst battles of the war. We went on to Mount Vesuvius just outside Naples. We were pulled out, leaving behind all our guns, ammunition, etc: only personal kit was required. We were back on the boat again, so nobody knew. Next port of call was Aden, then on to Felixstowe and you can guess the rest – the Normandy Beaches. It was get ready for another lot – we were gutted.

We were ordered to remove all our Eighth Army flashes, and sew on 30 Corps Africa Star Ribbons. We went on parade at Felixstowe and all the guns were waiting, not 25 pounders or self-propelled guns that we were used to but 5.5. and 4.5 inch guns. We had three days of very hard training: it was like driving a lorry instead of a mini. I landed in France with an advanced party, dumped in the sea on a steel mat, hoping that there was a gun crew there when we landed. We fired on the beach with open sights, then on to our gun position at Audrieu – the going was not too bad – then on to Fontenay. We were in action until we reached a place called Herent in Belgium where we rested for one week; the regiment then went through to Luneburg in Germany and was in attendance when Field Marshal Montgomery accepted the surrender of the German armed forces.

Ron Child's 21st Army Certificate and medals. The deed that earned him the Military Medal was to retrieve some very important maps from an armoured vehicle in St.Lo, Normandy, which had been bombarded by the enemy. Inside was a wounded soldier. Ron crawled out to the vehicle and reversed it out of the enemy's reach, saving the soldier and the maps.

Walter (Bill) Pike

Bill Pike lived with his wife, Lillian, in Downfield Road for many years and worked at the County Hospital from the 1930's until he retired in 1972, except for his war service. He was a very popular member of staff and often carried out tasks over and above his position as a ward orderly – his cheerful helpful manner was always a tonic for all the patients. Before and after retirement Bill went around the village giving advice and help to the sick, the elderly, and the housebound.

Below is his own account of time he spent in the Far East during the Second World War:

I was a medical sergeant in the 18th Division and taken prisoner at Singapore in 1942. Later on in the year I with thousands of others was sent to Siam (now Thailand) to build the "Railway of Death".

It was in May 1943 that I was sent to take over a small jungle sub-camp of about 600 men and 20 officers. This was called "Spring Camp" and was a very bad camp, situated away from the river and all water had to be drawn from a small spring. There were no huts for the prisoners, only ones for the Japanese. Bits of rag or pieces of old tent were stuck up with bamboo poles for the men to sleep under. There was no sanitation and no hospital; the men had no beds or blankets, few cloths and few boots. The diet consisted of 1lb of rice a day, peanuts or a small supply of vegetables.

We worked from dawn until dusk with each man having two tools, a pick and shovel, There were a great number of sick men, about 150 every day. The number of dysentery cases was very high, although most cases were malaria, bad skins and ulcers. The medical supplies were very poor. The Japanese issued a small amount of quinine. For dressings we boiled old dressings and any old cloth we could get hold of. I took over three small tents and made them waterproof; the men made me bamboo beds and the mattresses consisted of rice sacks filled with dry leaves.

I opened a small sick bay for the very sick and I managed to obtain about sixteen rice sacks to use as blankets. Bedpans and urinals were made out of bamboo wood, and leaves and dry grass took the place of toilet rolls. Three petrol tins were used for washing, no soap or towels were obtainable. The patients' loincloths were washed and dried and used to wash themselves, until these redried they would lie underneath a rice sack.

About the middle of June, cholera hit us and no one appeared to have seen it before. The Japanese Guards became very alarmed. I took charge of the cholera sick 'hospital' which consisted of about seven tents, 20 rice sacks, six empty petrol tins, four bedpans and urinals. There were few dressings and no intravenous sets. Patients were admitted day and night with vomiting and diarrhoea and, if they survived the first twelve hours, they stood a good chance of recovery. The very little treatment

140

Walter (Bill) Pike as a young man with his parents.

for them consisted of a few drops of iodine in water or a few crystals of potassium permanganate on rice paper to ease the hiccoughs after vomiting.

We collected and dried fresh leaves and grass each day and then placed them in the rice sacks for new admissions. As soon as a patient died, he was cremated on a large bonfire which was kept burning day and night. Isolation for all patients was one month, no stools were examined by us but they were later on in the year by the Japanese medical staff.

The medical officer in charge of the camp was Captain Richardson R.A.M.C. and we all owe a great deal to his leadership.

Bob Akers

I left school at 14 years of age after the outbreak of the war in 1940. First I joined the A.R.P. (Air Raid Precautions) as a messenger. My main job was to sit by the phone at Wren's bakers shop in The Street, now known as Downfield Road (as Mr. Wren was the Chief Warden) waiting for any messages about the air raids.

It was while on duty on the 19th April 1941 that we were shaken by a very loud explosion as if a bomb had landed outside. There was no sign of any damage, so I was sent out into the pitch dark, up to the Village Hall, the first aid post, where my sister Bonnie was a Red Cross nurse on duty that night. I was riding along London Road where I can remember being thrown off my bike by running over large lumps of mud. I reached the Village Hall and found the windows broken but no-one was hurt. I think they were concerned about me as I looked like a ghost, because the vibrations had blown the flour in the bakery off the shelves and I was covered in white flour. The explosion turned out to be a mine that had landed about 150 yards away down the Roman road, at the back of the garage. The following morning the entire village went to see what had happened, and found a very large crater just inside the field. It appeared that the parachute carrying the mine had not opened properly. I found the parachute cone, but the police took it away from me.

Bob Akers age 17 in The Fire Service

I can also remember a house in The Street being damaged by a stick of bombs, and others fell in the allotments which were then behind The Street in the fields beyond. One had not exploded and I saw the sappers of the Royal Engineers Bomb Disposal Squad defuse it. I think the Deard's family lived in the house. During another raid I was standing outside, near the church, when there was a swishing noise followed by a bang. A bomb had exploded in Dell's Woods behind the College, just missing the chapel. The story was that was an old Haileybury boy had been trying to bomb the dome!

During my time in the National Fire Service, there were competitions held in St. Albans Stadium to find the fastest crews, etc. and the best messenger team. We entered our team of four messengers three from Hertford Heath, myself, Tom Hudson, Digger Turner, and one from Hertford. We won the cup, which was presented to us by the local M.P.

We also used to spend some nights in Hertford Fire Station, located where Waters Garage is now. The firemen used to practice their drill on how to use the pumps over the Roundings on Hertford Heath, pumping the water out of the pond.

It was during one of these exercises, whilst an air-raid was in progress, that a V1 doodle bug came overhead. As it passed the engine cut out, and after a few moments the familiar explosion occurred, so we decided to go and see where it had landed. Reaching the junction of Mangrove Road from Elbow Lane, we could see smoke coming from the other side of the road, and a further 200 yards up the track we found a smoking heap, which was all that was left of a house. We heard the cry of a baby, so we dug with whatever we could. We then found a woman lying across the back of the settee completely naked and pitted blue, obviously dead. With more digging we found the baby in a pram covered in dust, and an old man sitting in a chair, luckily both were still alive. The V1 had dropped outside the backdoor and blown the poor woman through the house. The husband as it turned out was working at Waltham Forest munitions, doing night work. It was not long before more help arrived.

My next experience came whilst I was in the National Fire Service. We had a car and a pump, and our station was in the Townshend Arms. The leading fireman were John Howsen and Arthur Penn, some of the other fireman from the Heath other than myself were: Jim Phypers, Ernie Rickets, George Wilcher, Stan Bottrill, Charles Timpson, Ernie Timpson, Jack Mole, Ernie Ricketts, Arthur Chapman, Laurie Mynard, Henry Biggs, Joe Hillyard, Ron Turner and Tom Hudson.

One night during a raid, one of the incendiaries dropped on and around Foxholes had gone through the roof of one of the houses opposite the police station. As I was the smallest and the lightest, my fellow fireman lifted me up; I went into the bedroom and removed the bomb by throwing it out of the window. I found out later that some of them exploded when they were about halfway down, I was lucky!

On the 25th July 1944 whilst on duty at the station at the Townshend Arms in London Road, some of us were on the other side of the road when there was a noise and a flash from a house about 120 yards away, followed by a hell of a bang. I was blown to the ground. It turned out that the fire from the tail of a V1 (doodle bug) had struck the roof of a house in London Road and then landed in the allotments on the other side of the road, level to where I had been standing. What a near miss!.

Four weeks later, I was called into the Army and sent to Northern Ireland – after being in the Air Training Core for four years, training for the R.A.F. and being accepted for aircrew!

Tom Hudson

Tom Hudson was also in the fire service during the war from 1939 to 1945. Tom's grandmother's house was one of those destroyed by the doodlebug as it went over, landing in the allotments on the other side of the road. He also worked for a contractor carrying out emergency repairs on windows and roofs damaged by the bombs.

Tom was one of three children who lived in London Road, where he was born. He now lives in Trinity Road. He was once the Clerk of Works for Hertfordshire County Council, and has also worked at Haileybury College in the heating engineer's department for about eleven years before retiring. His mother also worked at the college in the laboratories during the war.

Tom remembers that Mr. Carter and his son used to bring milk round on a bicycle with milk containers on the handlebars one on each side. He would some times empty his bag and give away the farthings. The school master at that time was Mr. Thomas. He made you show your handkerchief before going in to the school and if you had forgotten it you were sent home to get it – a ritual that went on for many years at the local school. Tom also remembers having to run up Mount Pleasant to a house called the Snuggery and back to the school before being allowed to go in. A saying by Mr. Thomas, when we asked if we could play football, was "bring your boots on Spec".

There was also a boy's club held in Mr. Atherton's garage up the Roundings that Tom Hudson attended.

Jimmy Johnson

The following is an account of Jimmy's life by his wife Edna, née Warner:

He was christened Ernest but was always known as Jimmy to his friends. He was born in 1923 at no 7 London Road, called "the corner" of Church Hill, Hertford Heath. He was one of five children and a real country lad. He loved the Heath dearly, he talked of playing whip and tops on the road which was free from traffic in those days, except for Taylor's coal lorry and the milk horse and cart. The boys used to wait for the coal lorry to slow down at the bottom of Church Hill and then hung on to the back to get a ride up the hill, laughing and dragging their feet on and off the ground. Jimmy's family kept pigs, chickens and goats on waste ground on Church Hill. He had a catapult made of yew wood, with which he caught many a moonlight roosting pheasant. He also kept ferrets for netting rabbits, which made a good meal for the family.

He loved playing cricket for Hertford Heath in the 1950's, bowling was his great gift. They played in three different venues – the meadow along London Road, Carter's Farm in Downfield Road and what is now the Playing Field. Some of his friends were Peter Parker, George Watson, Squirts Turville, Podge Hornett and Snowy Childs.

I (Edna Johnson) was born in Hertford and at the time of our marriage in 1947 worked for Hertford Borough Council as a typist. We had two children, Christine and Marilyn, who went to the village school and were taught by Miss Knight, the same teacher who taught their dad She was a tower of strength to the school. Jimmy worked in the Lea Valley Nurseries growing tomatoes, cucumbers and flowers until he volunteered for the Royal Navy at seventeen and half years of age.

He served on the Russian convoys and spent five years on the battleship, HMS Howe, in the Pacific area where it was among the first ships to be dive bombed by the Japanese Kamikaze death pilots. He said he saw men with their flesh burnt off their bodies – it was a horrible experience.

When they were not in action, Jimmy was chosen to be the 'Captain's cabin hand' which he enjoyed. He always talked about the late King (George VI) coming aboard and he tried his hat on but it was too big for him. He treasured his bosun's whistle (which I still have) which used to pipe people aboard, or when they were leaving. He was also very proud of the "Burma Star Medal with Bar" and all the other medals relating to his war service.

Sailors from the Royal Navy came to play the pipes at his funeral in 2002. It was a very moving ceremony.

Peter Parker

Peter was born at 21 London Road, Hertford Heath. He was married to Gene Parker, née Turville, who also was born on the Heath, and they had four children, Christine, Lorna, Raymond (Ben) and Andrew. Gene currently lives in Hoddesdon but still has strong connections with the Heath as three of her children still live there. Gene was born in Downfield Road which in those days was called Ware Road. Pete and Gene went to school together in the local school. Pete's claim to fame was that he carved the words on the plaque for the planting of the cherry tree by the side of the College Arms, now called the Jolly Pindar. He had a black belt in Judo, and gave lessons to the local children at the Youth Club.

During the war he was a Gunner in the 147 Heavy Artillery, also the Surrey and Sussex Yeomanry, Queen Mary's Regiment. One of his war stories is about the Normandy Landings in 1944 on Gold Beach.

"We landed on Gold Beach, then went overland for 15 kilometres to Port-en-Bessen. It had been a hard slog from the beach to Port-en-Bessen. We had been there about three hours when we got a call from our HQ telling us to get our medical orderly to a field just up the road where some commandos from 47 Royal Marines

Fifty years later – Peter Parker's meeting in 1999 with the widow of his friend, Leslie Brockman.

Commando were trapped in a German mine field with many killed. Our medic went with others from more units in the area, but he was killed straight away by an anti-personnel mine – these mines when you disturb them jump up about three feet and explode. They are filled with about 30 half-inch ball bearings which can cut you in half, and this is what happened to my friend Leslie Brockman. He was aged 28, married with no children, cut off in his prime. We put him in a blanket before he was taken away on a cold and wet day on January 18th 1944 in Normandy.

"Fifty years later, my wife and I went back to Normandy to find his grave, and this we did in Bayeux Cemetery. On June 6th 1999, we went back for the 55th anniversary and while I was standing at his grave a little old lady came up to my wife, Gene, and said 'that's my husband's grave'. I put my arms around her and we both cried, it was a very touching moment for me, my wife, my son Raymond, and my grandson, Scott.

Memories of Mrs Edie Childs

I was a fire watcher, also a post woman during the war. Our headquarters were in the Village Hall. The warden was the late postmaster Mr. Williams.

I well remember the land mine falling on the Roundings. I was out with my daughter when we heard a droning noise overhead; we lay down flat, no sooner had we done so than the road was covered with slates, glass and rubble. Something touched my hand but I didn't take any notice. When we got home I found my hand was bleeding, I then realised how lucky we had been to have been outside instead of in. We found the gas had blown, windows were out and my dog which I had left inside had to be put to sleep due to shock.

The next day was Sunday and the men in the village were boarding up the windows and clearing the debris off the road. Our late constable, Mr. Pearman, was showing them the parachute which he had brought from the Roundings. The Village Hall was opened for lunches which you could buy for one and sixpence. I went down during lunch hour and played my concertina and collected money for the Red Cross.

The Grange on the Roundings was opened for bombed-out children from London sponsored by the Americans. They went to the Village School. They were visited by Mr. Roosevelt. Several of us got together and decided to arrange a concert party which we put on at the Village Hall. Haileybury College was very generous in lending chairs, etc.

Mrs M. Hunt took over adults assisted by Miss Gwen Fitch, also Mrs E. Timson trained the children which she was foster mother to during the war. She taught them dancing, wrote their sketches and made their costumes; they were great hits with the audience and were well patronised. Mrs. Bulley was our pianist and she also played her piano accordion. We put our concert on in several places outside the village. Mr. Hipgrave kindly let us have his lorry to take us around.

We had a Merchant Navy week, Mrs. Mole's daughter won the contest which was judged by Bobby Howes and his daughter Sally Ann. We were all very happy together and raised a lot of money for the war.

(Taken from the book *Pond Dipping*)

Rose Ansell's Story as an Evacuee

Rose Ansell (née Frater), one of six children was born in Islington, North London, and was an evacuee during the war and this is her story.

I have lived on Hertford Heath for sixty five years. I was ten years old when I came to the village. I was an evacuee, I can still remember being on the train, with all the parents standing on the platform waving to us and crying, we all waved back. We were happy; we thought we were going on an adventure. I was very lucky: I stayed at no 12 Woodland Road, Hertford Heath, with two wonderful people, named Arthur and Alice Penn. They were just like another mum and dad to me.

I never went straight home from school, I would go up to Portland Place with other girls to meet a wonderful lady named Mrs. Timson, who taught us to tap dance. Mrs. Bulley who played the church organ would play the piano for us, we formed a dance group and if there was a concert at the Village Hall, we would go along and take part. The hall would be packed. I always said Mrs Timson deserved a medal for giving up her time to us.

I never went back to London because I met Vic, my future husband, when I was sixteen. We met a one of the dances in the Village Hall, and we have now been married for over fifty years. Vic was born in the village and was the son of the local gamekeeper of Balls Park.

Rose and Vic Ansell

147

I think it's sad, but nobody seems to have a lot of time for a chat these days. In the old days everyone new everyone else in the village, now it is so built up, but people have got to have homes to live in.

There were many more evacuees sent to Hertford Heath other than Rose. One boy named Jack Stevens was looked after by Mr. and Mrs Leslie Wren and the brother Joe was looked after by Mr. and Mrs Charles Cox – both families lived in The Street (Downfield Road). Mrs Jean Bray's mother, Mrs. Turner, also cared for two evacuees during the war. Many will remember Fonto, another memorable evacuee, and Jimmy Tibbs who became Henry Cooper the boxer's corner man.

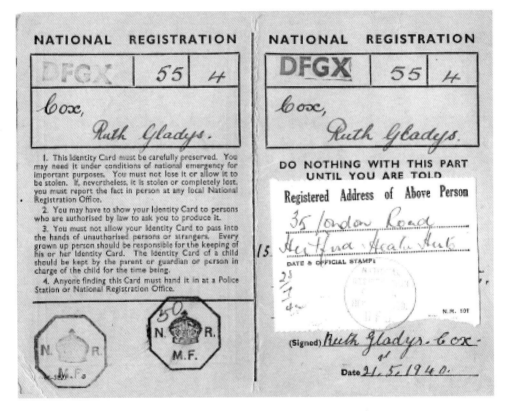

National Registration identity cards were issued to everyone during the Second World War. This one was issued to Mrs. Ruth Andrews, née Cox.

I WISH TO MARK, BY THIS PERSONAL MESSAGE,
my appreciation of the service you have rendered to your
Country in 1939.
In the early days of the War you opened your door to strangers
who were in need of shelter, & offered to share your home with
them.
I know that to this unselfish task you have sacrificed much
of your own comfort, & that it could not have been achieved
without the loyal co-operation of all in your household.
By your sympathy you have earned the gratitude of those to
whom you have shown hospitality, & by your readiness to
serve you have helped the State in a work of great value.

Elizabeth R

Mrs. C. Cox,

Two royal certificates awarded to the Cox family of Hertford Heath for their service in the Second World War.

Left: a certificate given to Mrs. Cox for taking in evacuees and signed by Queen Elizabeth II

Below: a certificate signed by King George VI given to Mr. Charles Arthur Cox for serving in the Home Guard – donated in memory of her father by Mrs Ruth Andrews of Downfield Road.

In the years when our Country

was in mortal danger

CHARLES ARTHUR COX

who served 18 April 1942 - 31 Dec.1944

gave generously of his time and

powers to make himself ready

for her defence by force of arms

and with his life if need be.

THE HOME GUARD

John F. Law

During the Second World War, John F. Law served in the local infantry regiment, the Beds and Herts, and went with the 1st Battalion to Burma as part of the Chindits special force. He died, aged 26, on the 9th October 1943. Those killed in Burma were buried in a cemetery there and each stone was photographed and given to the families.

John Law standing in front of the Old Vicarage in Hertford Heath and (right) his memorial stone in Burma.

Hertford Heath Men who gave their Lives during the Second World War

Noah Ansell, John F. Hawkins, William G. Craxford, Jim B. Hornett, Alfred G. Dickinson, John F. Hyatt, Robert L. Frank, John F. Law, Ernest Griffin and Sydney J. Ryder.

John F. Hawkins was serving in the Royal Navy aboard the battle-cruiser, HMS Hood, when she was sunk by the German battleship, Bismarck, during the Battle of the Denmark Strait on the 24th May 1941. She went down with virtually all hands lost.

Warship Week, 1942

Following huge shipping loses in the Battle of the Atlantic, major savings were needed to raise money for the cost of a hull for a corvette. A target of £55,000 was set and one of Hertford Heath's efforts was to sell calendars at 3d each during the week March 14th to March 21st 1942.

In the calendar, there are details of clothes that could be purchased for coupons.

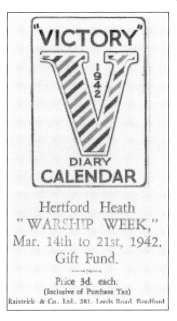

"VICTORY"
1942
DIARY
CALENDAR

Hertford Heath
"WARSHIP WEEK,"
Mar. 14th to 21st, 1942.
Gift Fund.

Price 3d. each.
(Inclusive of Purchase Tax)
Raistrick & Co., Ltd., 281, Leeds Road, Bradford

NUMBER OF COUPONS NEEDED.		
Women and Girls	A	C
Lined mackintoshes, or coats (over 28 in. in length)	14	11
Jacket, or short coat (under 28in. in length)	11	8
Dress, or gown, or frock—woollen	11	8
Dress, or gown, or frock—other material	7	5
Gym-tunic, girl's sk't w'h bodice	8	6
Blouse or sports shirt, or cardigan or jumper	5	3
Skirt, or divided skirt	7	5
Overalls, or dungarees or like garment	6	4
Apron, or pinafore	3	2
Pyjamas	8	6
Nightdress	6	5
Petticoat, or slip, or combination or cami-knickers	4	3
Other undergarments, including corsets	3	2
Pair of stockings	2	1
Pair of socks (ankle length)	1	1
Collar, or tie, or pair of cuffs	1	1
Two handkerchiefs	1	1
Scarf, pair of gloves or mittens or muff	2	2
Pair of slippers, boots or shoes	5	3
A—Adult.	C—Child.	

NUMBER OF COUPONS NEEDED.		
Men and Boys	A	C
Unlined mackintosh or cape	9	7
Other mackintoshes, or raincoat, or overcoat	16	11
Coat, or jacket, or blazer or like garment	13	8
Waistcoat, or pull-over, or cardigan, or jersey	5	3
Trousers (other than fustian or corduroy)	8	6
Fustian or corduroy trousers	5	5
Shorts	5	3
Overalls, or dungarees or like garment	6	4
Dressing-gown or bathing-gown	8	6
Night-shirt or pair of pyjamas	8	6
Shirt, or combinations—woollen	8	6
Shirt, or combinations—other materials	5	4
Pants or vest or bathing costume or child's blouse	4	2
Pair of socks or stockings	3	1
Collar, or tie, or pair of cuffs	1	1
Two handkerchiefs	1	1
Scarf, or pair of gloves or mittens	2	2
Pair of slippers or goloshes	4	2
Pair of boots or shoes	7	3
Pair of leggings, gaiters or spats	3	2
A—Adult.	C—Child.	

Hertford Heath Wings for Victory Parade 1943

The houses on the right of the pictures below were destroyed by the V1 flying bomb that fell in the allotments; the flame from the tail of the bomb caught the chimney of one of the houses and started a fire. The houses were burnt to the ground, the area was then known as the 'old bombed house' site until bungalows were built on the land. The families of May and Gwilym Williams, and Edward and Emily Hudson lived in the houses that were destroyed.

Among those in the parade were, Leading Fireman John Howsen, Digger Turner, and Bob Akers, from the National Fire Service, followed by the cubs and scouts some of whom were Ron Barwick, Jeff Mole, John Brown and Peter Porley.

The Women's Section of the British Legion, followed by ARP wardens.

The Scouts marching from College Road into London Road.

Uniformed organisations gather on the Village Green at the end of the parade.

Parades of this nature were held all over Britain. People were encouraged to raise money for the war effort, and to collect pieces of metal no matter how small for the purpose of building urgently needed aircraft. The programme produced for the parade in Hertford Heath (illustrated on the next page) shows that their aim was to raise money for the building of a Hurricane.

HERTFORD HEATH
Wings for Victory Week—
MAY 29th to
JUNE 5th, 1943

427

Price

2ᵈ

Hertford Heath Wings for Victory Week

THE HERTFORD HEATH WINGS FOR VICTORY WEEK COMMITTEE hopes that ALL in the Village will do their part in making a success of this effort. Our Target is

£5,000

to provide a

Hurricane

YOU BUY 'EM
THEY'L FLY 'EM

INVEST YOUR MONEY IN
NATIONAL SAVINGS CERTIFICATES
3% SAVINGS BONDS   3% DEFENCE BONDS
2½% NATIONAL WAR BONDS AND
POST OFFICE SAVINGS BANK

TAKE CARE OF THIS PROGRAMME !! It may win you a Prize. Lucky number will be announced at the DANCE on Saturday, June 5th.

Donations to Gift Fund may be sent to Mr. W. M. Williams, Post Office, Hertford Heath.

MAIN TARGET
for HERTFORD and
DISTRICT £160,000
OUR TARGET FOR
HERTFORD HEATH £5,000

Miss L. M. Camp, Heath Group, Target £11.
Mrs. J. W. Huxus, Hailey Group, Target £33
Mr. W. E. Williams, Schools Group, Target £45
Mr. G. Todd, Portland Group, Target £10
Mrs. M. R. Hunt, Langley Group, Target £65
Mr. J. F. Webb, London Road Group, Target £20
Mrs. H. King, Galley Hall Group, Target £10
Miss L. Pyle, Woodland Heath Group, Target £15
Mrs. J. Monk, Mount Pleasant Group, Target £15
Mrs. G. H. Jordan, Women's Institute Group, Target £30

Double Your Investment and reach the Top of the Tree

Programme of Events

SATURDAY, May 29th.
OPENING OF THE WEEK

SUNDAY, May 30th Parade by members of Civil Defence Organisations, A.T.C., B.R.C.S., Home Guard, Haileybury O.T.C., V.A.D., W.V.S. The Parade will march through the village, starting from College Road, to music by Haileybury I.S.C., J.T.C. Band, to an open air Service on the Village Green, at 11 a.m. Collection at the Service for the R.A.F. Benevolent Fund.

TUESDAY, June 1st. Display of Posters and Models ; Fancy Dress ; Doll Dressing and Dramatic Competitions ; Decorated Dolls Prams (girls), Decorated Trucks (boys), at the Schools at 3 p.m. Admission 3d, children 1d. Concluded by a Procession to the Village Hall (weather permitting).

WEDNESDAY, June 2nd. School children's Film Show by M.O.I., in the Village Hall, 2.30 p.m.

WEDNESDAY and THURSDAY, June 2nd and 3rd. Grand Variety Concerts, presented by the "Knitwits," in the Village Hall. Doors open 7 p.m., commence at 7.30 p.m. Admission, 1/6 and 1/-. Children half-price, must be accompanied by an adult. Tickets obtainable from members of the "Knitwits."

FRIDAY, June 4th. Whist Drive in the Village Hall at 8 p.m., organised by the Women's Institute. M.C.: Mr. J. Kirching. Tickets 1/-.

SATURDAY, June 5th. Grand Dance in the Village Hall at 8 p.m. Music by the "Victory Quartet." Admission 2/6. Members of H.M. Forces 1/6. Children under 16 not admitted. M.C.: Mr. R. Webb. Refreshments at popular prices.

154

CHAPTER NINETEEN

Some Old Cottages and the People who lived in them

The **Goat Cottages** were situated on the land now occupied by the Goat Public House car park and were called Goat Row. There were five cottages and the occupiers in 1901 were the families of Elizabeth Howes, Harry Judd, Charles Akers, Louisa Bradley, and John Gray. In later years other occupiers have been the families of: Jim Hornett, Bill Watson, and the Brown, Farnham and the Childs families. These families were re-housed in Woodland Road.

The Street Cottages (Downfield Road):
The Street was renamed Downfield Road in 1949 when the residents voted by plebiscite for the change. The cottages were situated on both sides of the road.

Hillcrest Terrace, Downfield Road:
There were five cottages and they are still in existence. The families that lived there in 1901 were those of: Charles Pavey, Alfred Barlow, George Webb, Alice Deards and John Catlin. In later years other occupiers have been the families of Pavey, Timson, Porter, Turville and Kiff.

The block of cottages that stood to the left of Hillcrest Terrace has been replaced by bungalows. The last one in the block was a cobbler's shop run by Mr. Prime.

On the other side of the Downfield Road just beside the Two Brewers Pub (now residential houses) was **Woodland Terrace.** It was nicknamed 'Stinkpot Alley' because the toilets and washhouse were at the end of the alley and was shared by the all the families that lived there. A water tank with one tap was the only source of drinking water. Some of the occupiers have been the families:

Akers, Judd, Brace, Brown, Maggie Smith, Grey, (Fanny) Wackett, Annie Shepherd, Soldier Smith, and Charlie and Maud Brace.

Left: Mr. and Mrs Charlie Brace standing outside their cottage in Woodland Terrace during the celebration of the Coronation of King George V in 1910.

There were three more rows of cottages in Downfield Road. One of them, called **Hawthorne Cottages**, has been replaced by council bungalows whilst the other two still remain.

Further down the hill in Downfield Road is **Downfield Cottage**, the former home of Rebecca Childs (George) and the Downs.

Pretoria Cottages near the pond:
These were on the left-hand side of the village green, leading to Pear Tree Cottage and were owned by Mr. Kemp who also conducted funeral arrangements. These

cottages have been replaced by modern bungalows. There were three cottages. Some of the occupiers have been the families of Penn, Phypers, Ward, Butterfield, Neal and Cutler

Pear Tree Cottage:

Martha Thurley was the occupier in 1901. From 1931 to 1938, William and Emma Randall were the occupiers. William Randall had been the accountant at Haileybury College for fifty-two years, and came back from his retirement on the Isle of Wight to spend the rest of his life in Hertford Heath. He and his wife are buried in Holy Trinity churchyard.

Church Terrace:

Built in 1887, these cottages form part of Mount Pleasant and are still in existence, stretching from the Old School to the church. The first cottage became a shop for a few years. Some of the occupiers that lived there in 1901 were the families of Daniel Hayden, John Pavey, Edward Bulley, Cornelius Cox, Benjamin Pratt, Isaac Smith, Henry Judd, Walter Phypers, George Childs and William Hill. In later years other occupiers have been the families of Barwick, Judd, Ansell, Foster, Childs, Camp and Cox.

New Zealand Cottages (Mount Pleasant):

These cottages were once owned by Edgar George who lived in the house nearby called Oakdene. The occupiers in 1901 were the families of Horace Gray, Charles Cox, Wilhelmina Streader and Charles Sibley. The end cottage was later occupied by George and Lillian Wilcher, who ran a smallholding at the back of it.

Edgar George had three daughters who are seen in the picture: Hilda standing, and Violet and Charlotte sitting in the garden of one of the New Zealand Cottages. They also lived in one of the cottages for a time. Charlotte on the right helped to run the Scouts in the village

Fir Tree Cottages (Mount Pleasant):

These cottages stood on land owned in 1846 by Captain John Townshend, although James Tristram occupied the part of the land called 'Haddy Croft'. The remaining plot was called 'Bush Hill'. Joseph Randall, a farmer from Jenningsbury, bought the land comprising about 2 rods and 24 poles for the sum of £26 in 1877. He had a dwelling house erected on the eastern portion of the land for his own use. Subsequently, he converted this house into three properties which were occupied by William Randall, Joseph Cox and William Cutmore. He also erected a new residence known as 'The Limes' on the western portion of land. When Joseph died

in 1897, the cottages were left to his wife, Eliza, and when she died in 1903 they were left to Joseph Prior, who was Joseph Randall's nephew. Since 1903 there have been a number of new owner/occupiers.

Jesmond Cottages (Church Hill):

These were built in 1913 by Edgar George, and four still remain. These were inherited by his daughter Violet. Some of the occupiers were the families: Akers, Lee, Grace Middleton, Mr. Hornett of the Salvation Army and Cook/George.

Church Hill:

There were five houses on the opposite side of the road from Jesmond Cottages but only two remain today. The families that lived there in 1901 were those of James Wilson, Eliza George, John Kiff, John Camp and Louisa Locking.

Sacrament Lane (Portland Place):

There were only five cottages in the lane in 1901 and the families that lived there were those of: Albert Barnes, Robert Cordell, David Bell, Fredk Pearce and Maria Hart. In later years other occupiers have been John Hayden, Brace, Gull, Sibley and Perrin

Vicarage Cottages:

There were six cottages in Vicarage Causeway, nicknamed "The Karsey" by the locals. Living there in 1891 were the families of William Camp, Sarah Croft, Elizabeth

Deards and Charlie Campbell. In 1901 they were lived in by Caroline Woodcock, Charles Bulley, Mary Cox, Harriett Kiff, John Nixon, Stuart Bruce and William Hayden. From 1927-1940 the Law family occupied one of the cottages.

May and Gladys Law standing at the front door of the cottage that was the first in the row, next door to the Mission Room. They were just two of seven children raised in the cottage.

Vicarage Causeway after a snowfall in 1932. On the left are Vicarage cottages. The spire of the Mission Room is in the distance.

London Road Cottages:

From the junction of Church Hill along London Road were eighteen cottages, built by Joseph Randall in 1877 at the same time as he built Fir Tree Cottages. He bought 14 poles of land for £525 and built four blocks of four and two semi-detached cottages.

The families that lived there in 1901 were those of William Phillips, Joseph Hornett, Edward Edwards, James Walford, Charles Pratt, Thomas Brown, John Saville, William Harrington, Frank Childs, Harriett Camp, Charles Camp, Emma Brace, Frederick Coles, Thomas Judd, Alfred Pavey, Edward Hudson, William Knight and John and Emily Huson.

During the Second World War on the 25th July 1944, the two semi-detached cottages were destroyed by debris from a flying bomb. The families that lived there at the time were Williams and Hudson.

Some of London Road Cottages as they were in the early 1900's.

The families that lived in the cottages from the Townshend Arms to the junction of Church Hill in 1901 were those of Alfred Wilson, Cornelius Meeks, William Camp, Herbert Morgan, James Pavey, Frederick Crane and Eliza French (The Shop).

The Old Post Office Cottages:
There are three cottages in London Road beside the garage. Two of the families that lived there in the 1930's were the Wilkinsons and Bartons. One of the families that lived there during the war was the Jackson family.

Top of London Road:
Ivy Cottage to the left of the College Arms was built by Matthew Campbell, an innkeeper of Hertford and first purveyor (or caterer) to Haileybury College. He built another cottage and a bakery behind it to supply the college. In 1829 he acquired a larger piece of the adjoining Heath and built Rose Cottage for himself. He gradually acquired more and more land, including Bride's Farm on the Roundings. *(Information found in C.M. Matthews' book 'Haileybury Since Roman Times').*

Elbow Lane:
A cottage built in Elbow Lane was also called Rose Cottage, and was the home for the gamekeeper to Sir G.F. Faudel-Phillips. Records show that from 1891 to 1914 the gamekeeper was James Matthews.

Priors Wood Road:
Priors Wood Road extended into what is now Postwood Green. The families that lived there in 1901 were those of George Bradford, Joseph Childs, Sara Westfield, Frederick Day, Daniel West, Henry Littleford and Hannah Howes. Others have been the Judds, Greys, Georges and Crofts. Some of these cottages were demolished and the families re-housed in Woodland Road.

Brickfield Cottages:
The two Brickfield Cottages were in Hogsdell Lane, formerly called Vicarage Lane. These were demolished to make way for modern housing. In 1891 the families that lived there were those of James Clark, police constable, and James Baldwin, mill-sawyer. Joseph Baldwin, mill-sawyer, and Thomas Stother, brick maker, lived there in 1901. None of these families were from Hertford Heath.

In 1940 the Law family moved into one of these cottages from Vicarage Causeway and the whole family worked in one capacity or another at the Vicarage.

CHAPTER TWENTY

Hertford Heath in the Kelly's Directories

These are extracts from The Post Office Directory 1855 and Kelly's Directories from 1890 to 1914. They detail the history and statistics of every village and town in Hertfordshire, including names of private residents and commercial businesses. Hertford Heath was detailed separately from Great and Little Amwell.

Little Amwell 1895

Formerly a liberty in the parish of All Saints, Hertford, Little Amwell was constituted as a parish for civil and ecclesiastical purposes August 2nd 1864 and is in the Eastern Division of the County, Hertford Petty Sessional Division, Union and County Court District, and partly within the Municipal Borough of Hertford, in the Rural Deanery of Hertford and Archdeaconry and Diocese of St. Albans.

The village stands on an eminence about a mile and three-quarters south-east from Great Amwell, and about 2 miles south from Hertford. The New River takes its rise in the parish or liberty, at Chadwell Springs, about 1 mile east from Hertford and is conveyed thence, as a monument on the spot records, to Islington, London, a distance of 40 miles. The church of Holy Trinity erected in 1863 by the Rev. David Barclay Bevan M.A., vicar here 1864-81, is a building in the early English style, consisting of chancel, nave, transept, north porch and an eastern turret containing one bell: there are 230 sittings, 125 being free. The register dates from the year 1864. The living is a vicarage, net yearly value £50 with glebe £38 and residence, in the gift of trustees, and held since 1881 by the Rev. Charles Wright Barclay M.A. of Trinity College, Cambridge. Here is a Mission Room erected in 1882, with 110 sittings.

The principal landowners are the Marquis Townshend, William Baines esq., and Francis Gosling esq., of Welbury House, Offley. The area is 526 acres, rateable value £2,655; the population 1891 was 843, of which 28 are in the Municipal Borough of Hertford.

Parish Clerk: Alfred Hayden (Mrs Dorothy Chalkley, formerly of Woodland Road, Hertford Heath, is the granddaughter of Alfred Hayden).

In **1902** Alfred Hayden is still listed as Parish Clerk.

In **1902** the principal landowners were Sir George Faudel-Phillips, Bart, of Balls Park, John Haines Jones Esq., William Perry Jones Esq. and Francis Gosling Esq. of Welbury House, Offley.
By Local Government Board Order 22,216, dated March 24th 1888, part of Amwell End in this Parish was transferred to Ware.
In **1914** the principal landowners were Sir George Faudel-Phillips Bart, of Balls Park, the Governors of Haileybury College and Robert Barclay Esq. of High-Leigh, Lord Street, Hoddesdon.

The Parish Clerk in 1914 was Walter Strange.

Little Amwell (continued)

1895: *National School (Mixed), for 230 children; average attendance, 210; William Chessell, master; Mrs Chessell, mistress; Misses Lavina Morgan and Christine Mitchell, assistant mistresses.*

In **1902** the headmaster and mistress remains the same, but the assistant mistress was Miss Shearman. The school was enlarged in 1894 to accommodate 280 children.
In **1914** the same details remain except that the assistant mistress was Miss Foster.

Private Residents Little Amwell

James Coleman	Rose Cottage, London Rd	1855
Rev. Charles Wright Barclay M.A.	Vicarage, Hogsdell Lane	1890/1902/1914
Joseph Chalmers-Hunt	Chadwell, Rush Green	1890/1895/1902
Henry Mitchell	Heathfield, Rush Green	1902
Samuel Sydney Carthew	Rush Green	1890
John George Rhodes	Rush Green	1890/1895
Rt Osmond McMullen	Rush Green Lane	1908/1914
Mrs Emma Damaret	Gamels Hall, Rush Green	1902/1908
Norman Chalmers Hunt	Gamels Hall, Rush Green	1914
Frederick George Gray	Wood Villa	1890/1895
Mrs Bamford	Lorne Villa, Mount Pleasant	1890–1908
Mrs Hughes	Lorne Villa, Mount Pleasant	1914
Joseph Randall	The Limes, Mount Pleasant	1890/1895
Mrs Eliza Randall	The Limes, Mount Peasant	1902
Edward Phillip Coleridge	The Limes, Mount Pleasant	1908/1914
James Day Thurley	No address	1890
Mrs Martha Thurley	Pear Tree Cottage, Mount Plsnt	1890/1895
Miss Thurley	Pear Tree Cottage, Mount Plsnt	1902
Gilbert Lyne	Pear Tree Cottage, Mount Plsnt	1908/1914
Mrs Ibbetson	Laurel Cottage	1890
William Thurley	Laurel Cottage	1895
Miss Elizabeth Thurley	Laurel Cottage	1902
William Randall	Laurel Cottage	1914
Edwin Thurley	Rushen, Mount Pleasant	19081914
William Randall	Fir Tree Cottage, Mount Plsnt	1902/1908
Edward Lyne	Oakdene, Mount Pleasant	1902/1908
Stuart Bruce	No address	1902
Isaac Warren	Hazelmere	1914
Mademoiselle Anet	No address	1914
Percy Cooper	The Downs, Downfield Rd	1914
Rev. Thomas Dawe M.A.	Woodrows, Mount Pleasant	1902
Misses Foster	Woodrows, Mount Pleasant	1908
Walter Denay	Woodrows, Mount Pleasant	1914

Commercial Little Amwell

William Baines	Farmer, Fishmonger. L.Amwell	1855
Henry Akers	Horse & Dray. The Street	1890/1895
Frederick Pamphlion	Horse & Dray. The Street	1901
Henry Warner	Beer Retailer	1902
James Ward	Beer Retailer	1908
Mrs Susan Brown	Brewers Arms	1855
James Childs	The Two Brewers	1901
James Childs Jnr	Beer Retailer	1890/1902/1908
William Henry Brooks	Farmer, Lime Kiln Farm	1890/1895/1902
Thomas Ballard	Townshend Arms P.H.	1855
James Childs	Townshend Arms P.H.	1890/1895
Miss Rebecca Childs	Townshend Arms P.H.	1902/1908
John Smith	Townshend Arms P.H.	1914
Francis Gull	Beer Retailer	1914
William Childs	Shopkeeper	1890/1895/1902
William Hayden	Shopkeeper, Church Terrace	1890/1895
Daniel Hayden	Shopkeeper, Church Terrace	1902
William Goldsmith	Shopkeeper, Church Terrace	1908/1914
Miss Eliza French	Shopkeeper, London Rd	1890/1902/1914
George Akers	Farmer, Rush Green	1855
William Gray	Farmer, Rush Green	1895/1902
William Thomas Cooper	Farmer, Rush Green	1908
William Thomas Cooper	Farmer, Rush Green	1914
Henry Brace	Shopkeeper	1902/1908/1914
John Parker	Lime burner Ware Road	1890/1895
Samuel Parker	Nags Head P.H. Ware Road	1890/1895
Joseph Parker	Nags Head P.H. Ware Road	1902
Charles Impey	Nags Head P.H. Ware Road	1908/1914
Henry Randall & Son	Farmers, Amwell Place Farm	1890/1895
William Chandler	Baker, The Street	1890
James Reed	Baker	1895
Ernest Walter Jaggs	Lusker & Corn dir The Street	1902
Jaggs and Edwards	Baker, The Street	1908/1914
Mrs Mary Ann Yates	Goat P.H., Vicarage Causeway	1890/1895
William Goddard	Goat P.H., Vicarage Causeway	1902/1908
Charles Marsh Pigram	Goat P.H., Vicarage Causeway	1914
Wm Chessell	Assist Overseer / schoolmaster Holmbury Villa	1895–1914
Charles Cox	Cab Proprietor	1902/1908
Alfred Hayden	Farmer, Newgates Corner	1914
Trustham King	Licensed Hawker	1914
Frank Robert Potkins	Shopkeeper, Mount Pleasant	1914
Thomas Henry Fitch	Builder, Mount Pleasant	1914
Henry Wadley, farm bailiff to	Mr. Joseph Rayment, Rush Green	1890
Charles Drummond	East Herts Golf Club (Sec)	1908

James Trustram	Farmer	1855
William Ward	Farmer	1855
Clarence Johnson	Draper	1908

List for Hertford Heath

Hertford Heath about 2 miles south-west, is a hamlet, partly in this parish and partly in Little Amwell liberty of Haileybury College, which is in the Heath, full particulars are given under the town of Hertford.

Woollen's Brook is a hamlet about 3 miles south-east; here is a Mission Church licensed for Divine Service and 75 persons, in which the vicar or his curate officiates; and there is a Mission Room in Hailey Lane seating 30 persons.

Parish Clerk: Frederick Parker **1895**

Post wall letter boxes, one near College Arms, and Hailey Lane.

National School (mixed) built in 1875 for 120 children; average attendance 81, Miss Kate Chamberlain mistress.

The master to follow Miss Chamberlain was Mr. Walter Plumer and his wife as assistant mistress. In **1914** Leonard Taylor is headmaster, Miss Thurgood infant's mistress. Rev W.J.Harvey M.A. the Vicarage correspondent. In 1914 there is the mention of a small chapel being built in 1900 by the Countess of Huntingdon's Connexion, erected as a memorial to Dr. Reynolds of Cheshunt College: it has 150 sittings.

Private Residents, Hertford Heath

Septimus Allen	No Address	1890/1895
Mrs Hyde	Heath House	1890
R.W.Bower M.A.	Heath House	1895
R.W.Bower M.A.	Rose Cottage, London Road	1902
George Thorold Waters M.A.	Rose Cottage, London Road	1908
Percy Richard Atherton	Rose Cottage, London Road	1914
Samuel Brown	Ivy Cottage, London Road	1890
	Boot Maker	
George Campbell	Ivy Cottage, London Rd	1890/1902/1908
Arthur Drummond Carlisle M.A.	Ravenscroft, London Road	1890/1895
Mrs Bachelor Russell.	Ravenscroft, London Road	1902/1908
Seymour Richard Cohley	Ravenscroft, London Road	1914
Arth.Drummond Carlisle M.A	Highfield House	1902/1908
Rev. Thomas Dewe M.A.	Highfield House	1914
James Warrell	Heathfield	1890
F. Gasper Dupuis	Heathfield	1895
George Burns	Heathfield	1902
James Frederick Murphy	Heathfield	1914
William Randall	Fir Tree Cottages, Mount Plsnt	1895

Ern. William Russell	Highfield Cottage	1890/1895/1902
John Moss Bell	Highfield Cottage	1908
Arnold Turner Jn B.A.	Highfield Cottage	1914
Thomas Simmons	Hailey Lodge, College Road	1890/1895
Horace Savory	Hailey Lodge, College Road	1899
Mrs Dixon	Hailey Lodge, College Road	1902
Rev Lionel Milford M.A.	Hailey Lodge, College Road	1908/1914
Henry John Lomas	Rosedeane	1902/1908/1914
Noel Roy Dalcour Tennant B.A.	White House, London Road.	1914
Alfred Richard Bailly	Bankside, London Road	1914
Albert Theodore Ford	The Woodlands, College Road	1914
Miss Walford	Harling, College Road	1914
Colonel Carmichael L. Young R.E.	Highwood, London Road	1908/1914

Commercial Hertford Heath

Albert Barnes	Poultry & egg dealer	1890/1895
Samuel Brown	Boot Maker, Woodside	1895
Mrs Eliza Campbell	Farmer Brides Farm, The Roundings	1890/1895
William & Henry Northern	Farmers Brides Farm, The Roundings	1902
Mrs Apling	Farmer Brides Farm, The Roundings	1908
Edward Apling	Farmer Brides Farm, The Roundings	1914
Andrew Cotton	Crown P.H., London Rd	1895
George Webb	Crown P.H., London Rd	1899
Mrs Sarah Webb	Crown P.H., London Rd	1902
Henry Wareham	Crown P.H., London Rd	1908
Henry Stephen Boreham	Crown P.H., London Rd	1914
Arthur Fletcher	Blacksmith, London Road	1890–1914

(In 1890 Arthur Fletcher is shown as being a blacksmith and Licensee of the Crown Public House).

Thomas Nottage	Greengrocer	1908
James Croft Barber	Shopkeeper, Priors Wood	1890–1908
William Gray	Builder, Saw Mills, London Rd	1890/1895/1902
George Gray	English Timber Merchant, London Rd	1908/1914
Charles Hugman	Fly Master (Horse & Carriage)	1890/1895/1902
James Campling	Fly Master (Horse & Carriage)	1908
Harry Huson	Cow keeper	1890 to 1914
George Ivory	Cattle Dealer	1890/1895
Henry West	Shopkeeper	1890
Trustham King	Shopkeeper	1895/1902
Henry A Hull	Sub Postmaster & Stationer	1908
James William George	Shopkeeper, London Road	1914
William Henry Ellis	Grocer, Post Office, London Rd	1914
William Mansfield	College Arms P.H., London Road	1855
John Brown	College Arms P.H., London Road	1890
James Tebby	College Arms P.H., London Road	1895

William Hillier	College Arms P.H., London Road	1899
John Brown	College Arms P.H., London Road	1901
Thos.Arth.Tulley	College Arms P.H., London Road	1902
John Henry Coulson	College Arms, P.H. London Road	1908
James Henry Moore	College Arms P.H., London Road	1914
George Webb	Beer Retailer, Havelock Arms L.Rd	1890/1895
Albert Henry Pearce	Beer Retailer, Havelock Arms L.Rd	1914
Henry Newland	Beer Retailer	1902
John Savill	Beer Retailer	1908
William Suckling	Hairdresser	1908
James Matthews	Gamekeeper to Sir G. F. Faudel-Phillips Rose Cottage, Elbow Lane	1914
Miss Newman	Butcher, London Road	1902
Walker Brothers	Butchers, London Road	1908
W. George Frogley	Butcher, London Road	1914
Henry Barker & Sons	Cab Proprietor and Motor Garage	1914
Alfred Close	Piano Tuner, London Road	1914
Mrs Jane Brown	Apartments, Springfield	1902
Mrs Elizabeth Ling	Apartments, Springfield	1908/1914
Henry Barker & Sons	Cab Proprietors and Job Master and Motor Garage	1914

Great Amwell 1895

Great Amwell is a parish and village, pleasantly situated on the declivity of a hill overlooking the Lea Valley, two and half miles north from Hoddesdon, a mile and a half east-south-east from Ware station on the Great Eastern Railway. Three miles east-by-south from Hertford Station in the Eastern division on the county.

The name Amwell is suppose to be a corruption of "Emma's Well", a spring issuing from the foot of the hill where runs the New River, which takes its rise at Chadwell Spring, about two miles west, in Little Amwell, uniting with a tributary stream a little below this spring.

The ancient church of St John the Baptist stands on the side of the hill.

Amwell Grove is the residence of Frederick Edward Lloyd Esq., J.P.

Mrs Spencer Charrington who is Lady of the Manor, Rev. Robert Scott Mylne, M.A. Henry C. Heard and the Council of Haileybury College are the principal Landowners.

1902 changes:

The council of Haileybury College is shown as Lord of the Manor. Amwell End formerly in this parish, under the Local Government Act 1894, was transferred to the town of Ware. Also under the provisions of the Divided Parishes Act, a detached part of this parish has been transferred to the town of Hoddesdon.

1914 changes:

The Council of Haileybury College remains Lord of the Manor and the Rev. Robert Scott Mylne M.A., Rector of Fartho, Northants, are the principal landowners. By Local Government Board Order No.47327, October 1st 1904, part of Little Amwell was added to Great Amwell civil parish and part of the latter to the former parish.

Great Amwell Private

Percy Arnold	Pepper Hill	1890/1902/1914
Phillip Edward Ash B.A.	Hailey House	1895
Frederick Bryant	River Cottage	1908
George Henry Chaplin	The Firs	1890/1895
Ernest William Chaplin	The Firs	1902/1908/1914
Rev. Henry Couchmann M.A.	Highfield House	1890/1895
Ernest Feiling	Amwell Bury	1890/1895
Basil Richardson	Amwell Bury	1902
Percy H Blythe	Amwell Bury	1914
John Wyman French	Hillside	1890–1914
Miss Gopsill	The Thrifts	1890/1895
Thomas Gopsill	The Thrifts	1902/1908
William Fredk Semple	The Thrifts	1914
Robert W Harrendence	Scott's Hill House, Warner Rd	1890/1895
Francis Olner Keysell	Scott's Hill House, Warner Rd	1914
Rev. William John Harvey, M.A.	Vicar, Glebe House	1890/1895/1902
Miss Mumford	Glebe House	1908/1914
Charles Henry Heard	Hailey Hall	1890/1895
Charles Yates	Hailey Hall	1914
Henry Jephson	Hailey Cottage	1890/1895
Charles Jephson	Hailey Cottage	1902/1908
Erle B. Randall	Hailey Cottage	1914
Captain Edward Kirkman Loyd	Springfield	1890/1895
Joseph Henry Turrell	Springfield	1902
Herbert Page	Springfield	1908
Edward Fredk Loyd, J.P.	Amwell Grove	1890/1895
James Shepherd	Amwell Grove	1902/1908
Charles B Lutyens	Amwell Grove	1914
Rev Robert Scott Mylne, M.A.	Home Lodge	1890/1902/1914
Thos Alexander Nash	Highfields	1890/1895
George Cooper/Mrs Glasspool	Highfields	1902/1908
John Moss Bell	Highfield Cottage	1908
Alfred Neale	The Grotto, Scotts Rd	1890/1895
Sydney Worpell Harrington	The Grotto, Scotts Rd	1914
Newman Mayo Ogle	Mylnfield	1890/1895
Francis Denham Marshall	Mylnfield	1914
Newman Mayo Ogle	The Cottage	1902/1908
Harvey Baldwin	The Cottage	1914
Mrs Parrott	Vicarage	1890/1902
Rev. William John Harvey M.A.	Vicarage	1908/1914
John Roderick	Filmer Cottage	1890/1895
Mrs Rolfe	Leigh Court	1890/1895
George Ward-Smith	Leigh Court	1902/1914
James Smith	Hailey Lane	1890/1895
David Whyte, Jnr. M.A.	Hailey Lane	1890/1902

Miss Mason	Hailey Lane	1902
Edward Culff	Hailey Lane	1908
Major Arthur Hoare	Hailey Lane	1908
Charles E.L. Ehrka M.A.	Hailey Lane	1914
Rev. Henry Charles Wright	Hailey Lane	1908/1914
Arthur Goodwin Stubbs	The Meads Cottage, Hailey	1914
Frederick Barry	Ravenscourt	1902
Henry Horn	Ravenscourt	1908
Ernest Beck	Ravenscourt	1914
Ethrayne Bicknell	Frogs Hill	1902
Miss Gant	Heathfield	1902
Alfred Naylor	Great Amwell House	1902/1908
Albert George Sandeman	Presdales	1902/1914
Thomas Barker	Hazeldene, London Rd, Ware	1914
Joseph Chalmers Hunt	Chadwell, Rush Green	1914
Joseph Henry Langton	River Cottage	1914
Alfred Naylor	Amwell House	1914

Great Amwell Commercial

Mrs Eliza Ambrose.	Laundress	1895/1902
Joseph Bangs	Beer Retailer, London Road	1895–1914
Frank Cheyney	Red House P.H London Road	1895
Stephen Smith	Red House P.H London Road	1902/1908
Henry Oliver Webster	Red House P.H London Road	1914
Elsden & Son	Photographers, Hailey Lane	1895 only
George Ford	Wagon & Horses P.H. Pepper Hill	1895/1902
Henry Piper	Wagon & Horses P.H. Pepper Hill	1908
William Starkey	Wagon & Horses P.H. Pepper Hill	1914
Henry Charles Heard	Landowner & Farmer, Hailey Hall	1895
Henry Huggins	Builder, London Road, Ware	1895
Dixon & Castle	Builders, London Road, Ware	1902/1908
John Dixon	Builder, London Road, Ware	1914
William Hunter	George IV P.H. Amwell	1895
John Hunter	George IV P.H. Amwell	1902
Fredk George Sulley	George IV P.H. Amwell	1908
John Watt Brown	George IV P.H.Amwell	1914
James Kent	Farmer Springle House, Hailey Lane	1895/1902
James Neve	Beer Retailer, Hertford Road	1895
George Neve	Beer Retailer, Hertford Road	1902
Mrs Jessie Page	Beer Retailer	1895
Frederick Page	Beer Retailer	1902
Mrs Sarah Page	Beer Retailer, London Rd, Ware	1914
Fredk Rowley	Farmer Sheepcotes	1895–1914
Mrs Susan Watson	Galley Hall P.H. & Shopkeeper	1895
Frank Watson	Galley Hall P.H. & Shopkeeper	1902/1908/1914
Edward Kingsley	Farmer Charlye Farm	1908

Jasper Weir	Farmer Amwell Bury Farm	1895
John Weir	Farmer Amwell Bury Farm	1908/1914
G.H. Chaplin & Co	Engine Packing manufacturing	1914
William Skipp	Nurseryman, Hailey Nursery	1914
Arthur Goodwin Stubbs	Nurseryman, Granville Nursery, Hailey	1914
Mrs Jane Wells	Shopkeeper, Mount Street	1908
Wm George Wells	Shopkeeper, Mount Street	1914
Septimus Warren	Poultry Farmer, Ware Rd, Hailey	1914
Henry Arth. Pearce	Boot man, London Road	1902
Alfred Watson	Builder, Ware Road, Hailey	1914

APPENDIX

Extracts from the Parochial Magazine

The following extracts from the Hertford Heath Parochial Magazine describe life in the village during Charles Barclay's time as Vicar:

January 1901

Twelve young men from our Village have been called to serve their Queen and Country in South Africa ... The School is now open, after its prolonged time of closing, owing to the outbreak of measles and diphtheria.

February 1901

There are 200 houses in the Parish and we have 198 subscribers, including a few who have left the Village ... The Men's Bible Class has re-opened at the Mission Room on Sunday afternoons. Mrs Barclay will be glad to enroll new members. There are at present seventy members.

June 1901

The Hertford Heath Football Club has since our last issue closed its season, which has been a most successful one. In connection with the East Herts League, 14 matches were played; of these 13 were won and one lost. 56 goals were obtained against 12. The team's ambition to win the cup was not quite so successful, as after going right through the season without defeat, they lost the last match to Rye Park. The cup will, therefore, be jointly held by Hertford Heath and Rye Park.

September 1901

Any favorable evening we are glad to welcome our friends at the Vicarage, if they are interested in astronomy. The view of the moon for the first time through the telescope always gives great pleasure, and causes astonishment when the mountains and volcanic craters are seen.

During the past hot, dry weeks, there has been some difficulty in keeping up the water supply, as there has been so little wind. The flow from the fountain has been maintained without fail, but unfortunately the reserve supply from the reservoir was used too quickly, laundry work in our village being responsible for this. Water for domestic use, however, is being drawn from the Vicarage tanks and so long as they hold out those needing water can have it in moderate quantities. We trust that ere these words are read that a few days wind may have removed all difficulty. The wind engine pump can raise nearly ten thousand gallons a day if it works continuously.

February 1902

The good old English custom of throwing rice over a bride seems in danger of being changed into a somewhat meaningless practice of scattering paper confetti in its place. The rice formerly was only thrown at the marriage of a farmer's daughter, and was intended to signify plenty, and is one of those delightful old customs we should be very sorry for it die out. The paper substitute would be very much better given up. It means nothing and it litters the churchyard for weeks, for it is very difficult to sweep away, whereas the rice is quickly cleared and much appreciated by our feathered friends.

December 1902

Village Library. If any of our friends have suitable volumes to give, we should be grateful for them. We wish to fill the library not only with books of a religious and helpful tone, but with good standard volumes, both of fiction and of general literature. We have already about a thousand volumes.

Water Supply. We have been singularly unfortunate this autumn with the Artesian well supply. Two months ago it became necessary, after nearly two and a half years constant work, to take the pump for repairs, and when it was replaced, after a week's work, it pumped about sufficient for the daily supply, but not enough to form a reserve. When, therefore, again a difficulty arose a fortnight ago, owing to fracture of the piston rod nearly 200 feet below the surface, there was again a short supply. We must ask our friends to show a little forbearance and not to vent their disappointment on the offending fountain-pump. It has come in for some hard treatment from time to time. If when the supply of pure water of the Artesian well is known to be short some care was exercised, it would last much longer; but when it is wasted, or taken for laundry purposes, it is soon exhausted, and those who need a small quantity for drinking have to go without. We are sure that a little consideration by our inhabitants would put this right; and we hope that if any person is seen doing wilful injury, some public spirit may be shown and the illdoer restrained. Fortunately during the failure of the wind engine pump, there was sufficient water in the Vicarage tanks to afford a supply to those who came for it.

January 1903

I have lately turned to some old lists of inhabitants of this parish which I used when I first came among you (1880) and have been very greatly struck to find how few living in those days remain: out of nearly two hundred households, only fifty-two and of these only twenty-four live in the same house as formerly. Three out of every four have passed on their way, and we know them no more, and suchlike changes are before us also. The greater number of those who read these works will, within the next twenty years, pass hence, it may be to other homes on earth, it may be to the long home above.

The Village Library at the Mission Room re-opens with the New Year, and we trust it will meet a great need in this place. Each Monday afternoon, at twenty minutes past four, books may be taken out, and also after Thursday Evening Service. A catalogue of the Library is enclosed in our Magazine for this month, and in it will be found the rules and also some useful hints to readers. There are many good standard books, and also a large selection of books of adventure, so much appreciated by the lads.

August 1904

The question of our Village Water Supply, which some six years ago we hoped was solved, is still with us and I greatly regret that just at the time when the Village tanks ran almost dry, that my Artesian well pump also ceased to act. I am glad, however, to tell you that it was the pump and not the water which failed us; but now having to remove the pipes I am making extensive improvements, not only replacing the tubes with those of much larger bore, and fitting a new pump of a superior kind, but I am putting up an engine to be used for working the pump when the wind is insufficient. This certainly ought to end all difficulties. And I cannot tell you what a pleasure it will be to me personally to see the children again freely drinking at the fountain, and all obtaining really good water with absolutely no stint. There appears to be no lack of water in the well, so that it is now upwards of 240 feet, and the water stands 45 in depth. I shall feel repaid if our difficulties are really at an end, and I trust our present inconvenience will make us value more highly God's good gift.

September 1908

A few years ago I made some suggestions with respect to the demeanor at funerals at our little Church. Many of you spoke to me with strong approval of what I then wrote and the result was much greater respect and decorum. But I fear that is being forgotten, so I will repeat what I then said. First, do not bring babies. At the last funeral I counted no less than seven babes-in-arms. They are very disturbing to the solemnity of this occasion. Next, discourage your children from coming unless they are mourners. It is very unseemly for children to be crowding round the graves and staring at the mourners. Then some attention should be paid to dress. If you come to a funeral, come to give your sympathy to the bereaved and to show some outward sign, just a black ribbon, if nothing more. The practice recently has been for some women and girls to come with no hats or any other preparation, apparently very often direct from the washtub. This is most painful and distracting to all and public opinion ought to make such a thing impossible.

October 1908

The Evening Cookery Class, which is again opened in the Mission Room, will be found excellent preparation for girls who are going out to service, as well as for home work. The food prepared is sold at cost price; a notice of what is to be had is put up on the Mission Room door each Friday.

December 1908

The laying of the Metropolitan Water Board's main throughout our village ends all difficulty with respect to the Water Supply either now or in the future. For many weeks I gave anxious consideration to the question whether or no I was right to promote the scheme and close my supply, for unless I undertook to do so the Board refused to lay the main. Taking all things into consideration I felt strongly that the welfare of the Village must not in any way be sacrificed by my own feeling of disappointment at no longer having the pleasure of supplying the water. A continuous supply to every house will prove an inestimable boon and I feel convinced that had we refused it now, when the opportunity arose, we should long regret doing so.

As I said in my statement, lately sent round to all whom it concerned, I feel grieved at the expense falling on some who can least afford it. I have sought to look at the matter from every point of view, not the least important being the future. Some may remember ten years ago I made the promise that in the event of my leaving the Parish I should make over my Artesian well and all the apparatus to the Parish Council, but ten years' experience has shown me that the pump, engine, etc. require very much more attention than I had supposed, and I can see that the Parish Council would have had great difficulty in coping with it, for it needs a man working on the spot. Besides, my own knowledge of mechanics has saved many a costly bill for repairs.

I feel sorry that the Water Board will not lay on a supply to the drinking fountain. They fear that if they do so many owners would refuse to lay on the water to their houses, but as soon as they are all connected up they will consider the question.

January 1909

Although such long notice was given as to the date when the Vicarage water supply would cease, many owners have as yet taken no steps to have their houses connected to the main. As I understand that in many cases they do not intend to do so until my supply is cut off, I feel I must abide by what I said and cease definitely my supply on January 1st. I will endeavor to leave off with the tanks filled which will afford drinking water for some time, if the users of it are careful and obtain their water for household purposes from the old pump.

June 1909

Again this year we combined the observances of May Day and Empire Day. The children marched down from School, led by young Mr. Russell on a pony, in a herald's dress and blowing a horn. At the rear of the procession came the May Queen on a black pony surrounded by her bodyguard and maids-of-honour. A very large number of people were gathered in the Vicarage grounds. On arriving at her throne, decorated with flowers, she dismounted and was crowned with a wreath of apple blossom. The programme, which was a very full one, was promptly entered on, consisting of the National Anthem, various patriotic songs, dances by the children round the maypole and various other old English pastimes.

December 1910

The Coal and Clothing Club. I have not yet mentioned in our Parish magazine the Coal and Clothing Club which many of our friends find to be of great convenience and help. I have lately paid out the funds in hand in the form of tickets for coal or clothing, which are especially acceptable at the beginning of the winter. This year no less than 214 persons have been paying in and the total sum amounts to £188.10s.11d. while tickets to the value of £200.7s.10d. have been issued. On the coal supplies I made a reduction of one shilling a ton, but this is not the only benefit which members receive, for buying the coal in large quantities I can get it at a considerably cheaper rate than if I purchased a little at a time. Then also to most of the tickets for clothing I make an addition, but no specified sum is promised, for if those who paid in most obtained the greatest benefit, as in some clubs, it would mean that the neediest obtained the least help. In addition to the above, assistance is given from the Haileybury Sacramental

Alms in the form of tickets which are taken in payment to the Club as representing half-a-crown. Several of our members who receive these tickets have informed the College ladies, who so kindly give them out, that I require an extra payment of one shilling a ton from those who have them. It is surely needless for me to say that this is altogether untrue.

July 1914

I have long felt that a very great want in our parish has been some system of sick nursing. I know well how much help a next-door neighbour gives in so many instances, but what is required is something more, the skill of a thoroughly trained and competent nurse. I am glad to say that I have been able to make arrangements with the District Nursing Association for Hertford, which will send to us a nurse from time to time on the application of the doctor attending the case. The scheme cannot be actually set on foot till September, so that I shall be able in the September number of our Magazine to give further details with respect to it. Naturally the Association will look for financial help from us and I am in hopes that we may be able to raise about £20 a year for the purpose. There are many well-to-do people in our parish who make no contribution to the work of the Church or to any of the charities. Perhaps this will appeal to them more than gifts for more direct religious purposes.

THE WAR

Amid all our parochial works and home duties, the great fact of the war is ever before us. It overshadows and seems to dominate all our thoughts. We have been from time to time cast down as we read of grievous losses, but we know that we are fighting on the Lord's side and we can thank Him for the honour He has entrusted to the British nation and we feel assured that the great military power of Germany will be destroyed. It seems very strange to us to read of villages in which no interest is taken, no help sent, no young men enlisting, no prayers offered up for our gallant soldiers. Since our magazine was last issued, several more have gone out and now we have 70 representatives serving their King and Country. May God bless, preserve and keep them, enable them to do their duty as British soldiers ever do and return in safety, their great work accomplished.

December 1914

We have had a very strong reminder of the war lately in our midst. Nearly seven hundred soldiers and officers of the 2nd North Midland Brigade were billeted in our village on November 16th. Most of the houses taking in their share. Colonel Sir Hill Childs with his adjutant and two other officers and a good many men had quarters at the Vicarage. They appeared to be marching on to the East Coast owing to disquieting rumours. The war continues its dread course with its hideous slaughter and terrible suffering. The whole outlook of all classes of society seems completely changed; we can scarcely imagine being carried back to the state in which we were living four months ago. All our various interests and anxieties seem so small compared with the greatest catastrophe the world has ever known. One great fact stands out, that our British soldiers have fought splendidly; they know that they are fighting for the right and for the honour of England and they are willing to give their lives freely for the welfare of their King and Country.

December 1918

The glorious, overwhelming news of victory overrides almost all other thought. That which we have fought for, longed for, prayed for, suffered for, is now, thanks to Almighty God, an accomplished fact. The moment the assured news of the signing of the Armistice came through on that great Monday, November 11th, notice was spread that we would gather in Church for a Service of Thanksgiving; and our little Church was, I am thankful to say, filled with worshippers and our prayers and thanksgivings went up from all hearts.

September 1919

It is a great pleasure to record the full and complete success of the welcome given to our returned Soldiers and Sailors on August 9th. The organising Committee acted well together, with never a discordant note, determined to give our men a thorough and hearty welcome. Mr. W Fitch, the energetic Secretary, evidently worked in the matter *con amore*. Although the collections made for the Peace observance were so recent, yet there was no holding back the ready and willing gifts, and I understand that our collectors' work was a pleasure such as collectors rarely experience.

The proceedings commenced by the gathering of our servicemen in the London Road, whence they marched down in full order to our little Church, the numbers so large that nearly three-quarters of the space was occupied by our gallant men. Then the Church filled up to its full capacity, many standing in the porch and outside.

November 1920

A public meeting has been held at the Mission Room to reconsider the question of erecting a Memorial Cross for our village. It will be remembered that last year when the beautiful brass was put up in our Church, some discussion took place with regard to a Cross, but there was a difference of opinion as to the place and also the material, and eventually it was dropped. The sum remaining after the brass plate had been paid for was voted to the fund for the expenses of the new addition to the Churchyard. By the vote of the meeting it was now unanimously agreed that a stone Cross should be erected on the Triangle near the Townshend Arms, and that the balance which had been voted to the Churchyard Fund should be re-transferred to the Memorial Fund. With respect to the Memorial Cross, Mrs. Barclay, who gave a most delightful talk at the meeting, undertook to make up all that was needed for the Memorial. But further subscriptions will be very heartily welcomed. We hope that the Cross may be finished and placed in position before we leave. It will be an exact copy of the Cross of St. Martin at Iona, and have the names of all who fell in the Great War carved in relief. It affords the opportunity of adding the names of the three who have died of wounds since the Brass Memorial was erected – William Bulley, Charles Pratt and Albert Croft.

The position of the Cross, in the opinion of all, is the very best possible. Placed at the entrance of our village, facing down the Hertford Road it will form a very conspicuous object and will serve to remind us all, whenever we pass by, of these gallant men who gave their lives that we might live. The names now number no less than 34. On the pedestal is a short inscription, together with the sacred words – "Greater love hath no man than this that a man lay down his life for his friends."

If you thought we have had hard winters in the past this must have been one of them, look at Downfield Road before and after the clearing of the heavy snow in 1940.

Before (above) and after a great deal of hard work with shovels (below).

Index

178

Hurrell, Miss Susan 44
Huson, Harry 25, 26; John 62, 72; Miss 99; W.E. 25
Huson's Farm 74
Hyatt, John F. 150

identity cards 148
Imperial Services College 19
Initial Teaching Alphabet 46

Jackson, Gladys 61; Sid 72
Jacobs, Richard 58
James, Chloe 7
Janes, Mrs. D. 54
Jenningsbury Farm 74
Jeremie, I. A. 39
Jerrard, Mr. 20
Jesmond Cottages 158
Johns, Elsie 101
Johnson, Billy 103; Jimmy 79, 93, 94, 144; Mrs. Edna 144; Professor Francis 25; Trevor 107
Jolly Pindar public house 16
Jollyman, Jo 100; Peter 73
Jones, Denise 102; Francois 109; Tina 97
Jordan, James 135, Mr. & Mrs. 70; Nancy 99; W. 89
Judd, Bubbles 43; Christine 110; Daisy 102; Jean 110

Kanolty family 96, 111
Kemp, Mr. 156
Kerr, Ernest & Jean 102, 124
Kershaw, Mr. 26
Kiff, George 116; Len 7, 69, 70
Kilminster, George 69
Kimpton, Bill 126; Bob 69, 90, 126; boys 85, 97; Pam 54, 96 *and colour pages*
King, Dave 107; Lou 92, 103, 104, 119, 126; Mr. G. 71
Kissing Gate Field 79, 80, 90
Kitching, Alan 103, 104; John 52; Ken 43, 109; Roy 71
Knight, Miss 45, 144

Ladies Circle 100
Lambert, Mr. 49
Langman, CSM Bert 20
Langman, Janet 99; Pat 109, 110
Law family 43, 150, 159
Leader, Mark 106; Simon 106
Leafy Oak Wood 65
Lebas, C.W. 39
Lee, Charlie 83
Lemprière, Dr. 8, 49
Lewis, Edna 92, 99, 109, 110; Eric 92, 109
Lightening Oak 19
Little Amwell Parish Council 130
Locking family 20, 30, 96, 119
London Road 15, 24, 26, 41, 44, 49, 59, 66, 67, 69, 70, 75, 77, 80, 114, 119, 129, 137, 160
Long Meadow 90, 103
Longmore, Philip & John 130
Lyne, Mrs. 62, 63, 79

MacCallan, A.F. 95
MacCorkindale, Simon 19
Macer, Dominic 106
MacLean, PC 125
Madden, Rosa 111
Malthus, Rev. T.R. 18
manslaughter 116
Marshall, Bishop 103; Ian 103
Martin, Arthur 74; Sir Clive 19
Mary, Queen 24
Mascall, Edgar 54
maypole dancing 43, 47
McBean, Teddy 94
McCarthy, John 19
McGinty, Shirley 105
Mead, Vera 99
Meals on Wheels 124
Meekins, George 54
Memorial Cross 31, 181
Merck, Sharpe & Dohme 9
Miles, Dora 119; William & Christine 71
milk deliveries, 72-73
Mission Room 28, 38, 48, 98, 101, 102, 159, 160, 171, 172
Mole, Barbara 43; Jack 142; Jeff 152; Wilf 104

Quitchell's oak 19